Authentic Selling®

Authentic Selling®

Be Real to Seal the Deal

Kendrick Shope

WILEY

Copyright © 2025 by Kendrick Shope. All rights reserved.

Published by John Wiley & Sons, Inc., Hoboken, New Jersey.
Published simultaneously in Canada.

No part of this publication may be reproduced, stored in a retrieval system, or transmitted in any form or by any means, electronic, mechanical, photocopying, recording, scanning, or otherwise, except as permitted under Section 107 or 108 of the 1976 United States Copyright Act, without either the prior written permission of the Publisher, or authorization through payment of the appropriate per-copy fee to the Copyright Clearance Center, Inc., 222 Rosewood Drive, Danvers, MA 01923, (978) 750-8400, fax (978) 750-4470, or on the web at www.copyright.com. Requests to the Publisher for permission should be addressed to the Permissions Department, John Wiley & Sons, Inc., 111 River Street, Hoboken, NJ 07030, (201) 748-6011, fax (201) 748-6008, or online at http://www.wiley.com/go/permission.

Trademarks: Wiley and the Wiley logo are trademarks or registered trademarks of John Wiley & Sons, Inc. and/or its affiliates in the United States and other countries and may not be used without written permission. Authentic Selling is a trademark or registered trademark of Kendrick Shope, LLC. All other trademarks are the property of their respective owners. John Wiley & Sons, Inc. is not associated with any product or vendor mentioned in this book.

Limit of Liability/Disclaimer of Warranty: While the publisher and author have used their best efforts in preparing this book, they make no representations or warranties with respect to the accuracy or completeness of the contents of this book and specifically disclaim any implied warranties of merchantability or fitness for a particular purpose. No warranty may be created or extended by sales representatives or written sales materials. The advice and strategies contained herein may not be suitable for your situation. You should consult with a professional where appropriate. Further, readers should be aware that websites listed in this work may have changed or disappeared between when this work was written and when it is read. Neither the publisher nor author shall be liable for any loss of profit or any other commercial damages, including but not limited to special, incidental, consequential, or other damages.

For general information on our other products and services or for technical support, please contact our Customer Care Department within the United States at (800) 762-2974, outside the United States at (317) 572-3993 or fax (317) 572-4002.

Wiley also publishes its books in a variety of electronic formats. Some content that appears in print may not be available in electronic formats. For more information about Wiley products, visit our website at www.wiley.com.

Library of Congress Cataloging-in-Publication Data is Available:

ISBN 9781394254057 (Cloth)
ISBN 9781394254897 (ePub)
ISBN 9781394254903 (ePDF)

Cover Design: Paul McCarthy
Cover Photo: Mia Farrington

SKY10098570_021725

My beautifully brilliant Halianna,
This journey that created Authentic Selling® was started by you, for you, because you deserved a role model for a mom who believed in herself enough to follow her dreams. Don't quit on your dreams, they are out there waiting for you. I believe in you, and I believe in your dreams.
"I love you, Mom"

Contents

	Authentic Selling® Orientation	ix
1	Your Authentic Selling® Mindset	1
2	Your Customer's Money	15
3	Authentic Truths	31
4	Your Authentic Business	47
5	Your Authentic Communication	63
6	Your Authentic Sales Conversations	77
7	Your Authentic Close	91
8	Your Authentically Written Sales Page Copy	109
9	Your Buyer's Brain	161
10	Your Authentic Business Plan	185
	Acknowledgments	207
	About the Author	211
	Index	213

Authentic Selling® Orientation

Hi Gorgeous Genius, you may be tempted to skip this introduction. I understand, believe me; I am someone who likes to jump in and get going, too. But one thing you will learn about me early on is that I am direct, and I'm going to shoot you straight so that you have less confusion and faster success. It's true, that being blunt can sometimes come across as harsh, but the purpose in this book is to bring greater clarity and reduce confusion. And let's be real, and bold is hot, y'all! This is more than a simple introduction. This is your orientation to Authentic Selling®. One of the things that makes Authentic Selling® unique is the way it is taught, in a "step-by-step" linear process. Don't test me because it's nothing for this nearly 50-year-old to break out into song with some New Kids on the Block "Step-by-Step," y'all!

There are nearly 20 educators in my family including teachers, principals, directors of schools, school board members, and even presidents of universities. I've been around teaching my whole life.

What's any of that have to do with you?

I'm glad you asked! It means that the way that I teach Authentic Selling® is very much like a fun class and you will learn proven tools, processes, and strategies that you have never heard before no matter your comfort level with selling. In fact, even seasoned salespeople who have studied sales most of their whole adult lives share that learning Authentic Selling® helped them find and close more clients and make more money.

Trust is a big freaking deal to me personally, and I'm going to ask you to trust me along this process. I'm as sure as my hair is red it's all going to come together in the end to make sense. You're going to have a process that is proven, allows you to stay within your integrity, not be a sales bully, and that works. Your learning starts here with the orientation. There are tools included in this orientation, including Your Fabulous Four, that will make the way you talk about your products and services easier.

If you've ever:

- Struggled when someone asked what you do, it is imperative that you read this orientation.
- Wondered how to show your expertise without sounding braggy or arrogant, this orientation is for you.
- Wanted to get people's attention so they trust you without waiting weeks, months, or years to build that trust, keep reading this orientation.

Let's start with some Authentic Selling® confessions and get some items out of the way. Besides who doesn't love a good secret? Don't get too excited, the juicy ones come later after we get to know each other a bit more, but be prepared, this book is full of great confessions – like the story of wanting to be a sex dancer when I was five, or the one where I sold drugs (the legal kind, y'all!), and how New Kids On the Block changed my life. And that's just the beginning.

You might be thinking, "I thought this was a book about selling?" It is! But darlin', if this experience can't be entertaining and educational at the same time, what's the point? We have enough boring sales books, and for that matter, boring business books that all sound the same. As sure as my hair is red, this book will not be a snoozer.

Instead, I predict you will laugh out loud. You may suffer second-hand embarrassment for me at times because I excel at making mistakes, and most importantly, you will learn how to get anything you want in life . . . read that again. Authentic Selling® will teach you how to get anything you want in life.

Where were we? Oh yes, let's clear the air about a few things before we jump in with some Authentic Selling® Confessions.

Authentic Selling Orientation

An important Authentic Selling® Confession #1: I have diagnosed Attention Deficit Disorder. I've been told that the inside of my head would look like "herding cats!" So why do you care that I have ADD? Well, I simply want you to know I will go off topic from time to time, but I will find my way back, so enjoy the ride.

Authentic Selling® Confession #2: As a Southerner, my first instinct is to greet you with a hearty "Hey y'all! How are you doing? Grab a glass of sweet tea before we start, and let me take a moment to thank you for choosing this book."

What Comes to Mind When You Think of Selling?

Is it a guy with a fake tan, too much mousse in his hair, and a cologne cloud trying to get you to buy a new car you don't want? Or maybe it's someone on Facebook inviting you to "parties" with essential oils, fancy underwear, or special knives that you *absolutely* don't want? Yep. Been there.

I promise this book is going to change the way you sell and think about selling. By the time you read the last page, it is likely you will enjoy selling and close 80–90% of every call you make with your ideal clients. I know you will be successful if you use the techniques in this book because those are the same techniques that have worked for thousands of entrepreneurs, business owners, and salespeople on multiple continents.

Gratitude

The first foundation of Authentic Selling® is that most every tool you're going to read about begins with gratitude. You will learn more about this in a later chapter but for now let me say thank you for taking your time and spending it with me. I understand how valuable that time is, and I assure you, this is going to be an experience, not just a book.

Authentic Selling® will teach you not only how to get rid of the old pushy way of selling, but you will learn how to get what you want more of in life. Umm, sign me up for more of what I want and less of what I don't. While we are on the subject, all this talk about balance drives me bananas.

Life Balance? Umm, No Thanks

"I just want to live while I'm alive."

— Bon Jovi

Seriously, I don't want balance, I want the scales to tip my way and give me as much of what makes me happy and as little of what I loathe as possible. Balance? Gross. Give me an unbalanced life with my family, money, NYC, and happiness tipping the scales toward unbalanced . . . oh and shoes and shopping, I want to add those to the unbalanced side, too. Yeah, shoes and shopping, and Broadway musicals. Okay, if you want to take a few minutes to jot down how you want to get unbalanced, go ahead; I'll wait.

Money and Time

Often people share they are short on two things: money and time. Time you can't make more of. So this book is going to be intentional with every second of your time! Inside this book, Authentic Selling® is going to teach you how to make more moolah! Now I know that many experts, books, and products promise to help you make more money but unless it's a book about selling, those promises are not the full story. Speaking of money, we need to introduce you to Authentic Selling® Truths and Authentic Selling® Pro Tips.

Spoiler Alert → This first Authentic Selling® Truth is one that you must understand for Authentic Selling® to work in your business and life.

Authentic Selling® Truth → The actual definition of the word *selling* is "the exchange of money for a product or service."

Authentic Selling® Pro Tip → Whenever I'm trying to understand and reframe my ideas about something, I first need to figure out what exactly is the actual meaning of this thing that makes me feel gross, which is why I went to the definition first.

Read that again: **The dictionary definition of selling is: "The exchange of money for a product or service."**

Were you surprised to read that? When I first looked it up, I was shocked because the definition seems simple and no sales bully required. I don't know about you but I hand over my debit card to pay for stuff every day. And I rarely feel icky, sleazy, slimy, or gross about any of those transactions. I mean, come on. Let's be real. When you go to Starbucks, do you cringe inside when you hand over your credit card in exchange for a latte? Or when you pay your hairstylist or barber to cut your hair? Yep. Didn't think so. When you really think about it, what is so icky, sleazy, slimy, or gross about selling? What's pushy about getting paid to give someone a product or service they need? We feel like selling is icky, sleazy, slimy, gross, crusty, musty, or dusty or at least uncomfortable because every single one of us has had a bad sales experience, spending too much time in that overly air conditioned room freezing our butts off waiting for the car salesman to just let us buy the damn car we want already instead of listening to him try and convince us that a fancy warranty is essential or that we should buy the more expensive model. There's a lot of negativity around selling, which is why we're going to start by getting crystal clear on what selling is and what selling isn't.

Well, here's the thing, negative connotations go WAY back in history. Way back in the day, traveling salespeople would come into town and offer up elixirs that promised the moon. Imagine someone walking up to you with a bottle in 1800-whatever and saying that you would feel like a teenager again if you bought it. Like most of our ancestors, I'm guessing you might have bought what that person was selling. But what was in those magic elixirs was something we still have today: alcohol. So while the sales proposition was true – people *did* feel like teenagers again for a while – they also felt terrible the next day. And when everyone's hangovers showed up . . . the salesperson was already on their way to the next town.

Of course people felt swindled and scammed.

Authentic Selling Orientation

That's why many of us feel icky, sleazy, slimy, or gross when we are on a sales call, centuries later.

As a culture, we have learned to be skeptical or negative about sales because everyone's grandma's grandma's grandma bought some elixir and felt the same way we did back in college before we learned the hard way about hangovers. Isn't that crazy? Though I will say that all the cologne some modern-day salespeople wear doesn't help, y'all.

You have my permission to drop the story about selling being bad. Because I don't know about you but I haven't been approached by anyone on a horse talking about magic elixirs lately.

The great news is selling doesn't have to feel icky, sleazy, slimy, or gross, and with the Authentic Selling® Tools throughout this book, selling will feel totally different. In fact, I would challenge you to reframe that icky feeling you may have regarding selling and think about selling a new way. **Selling is helping.** Your business is meant to make a positive impact on the lives of your customers; however, it's challenging to reach your people if you're using sales strategies that feel pushy.

The First of Its Kind

Authentic Selling® is not about perfection; it's about being genuine and true to yourself. Your Authentic Selling® Sales Guardrail (I'll talk about this in Chapter 1) is always available to help you do a check-in with yourself to make sure you're honoring what is genuine to you as an individual. In fact, the ability to check in with yourself is one of the things that makes this process unique, like you. It's the first sales system of its kind that provides a tool for you to do a self-check so you can make certain you are within your personal integrity. It's able to be adapted to different people's comfort level so that you never have to do anything that feels off. A perfect example of what makes Authentic Selling® uniquely customizable is that all of the different options that you will learn in later chapters are adaptable to you to work through objections and close sales. Some of the options are less direct while others are super direct.

Your Fabulous Four

Inside of Authentic Selling®, you will find custom proprietary tools created by me to help you do more of what you love and make more money. Now, we're going to get into that really in-depth later, but first, you're going to learn your first Authentic Selling® Tool. Your Fabulous Four is a series of five questions asked in four steps to help show your prospect who you are, what you do, why they can trust you, and why it matters, without being braggy.

Why Your Fabulous Four Matters

You can use Your Fabulous Four in two situations. First you can use Your Fabulous Four to shine a light on your expertise when you're selling your products and services. One of the biggest hurdles you will face when selling anything is the lack of trust that exists between seller and potential buyer.

When you share Your Fabulous Four in your marketing, you establish trust as an expert and become more likable to your prospects, which increases your chances of making a sale.

You can also use Your Fabulous Four when you are the buyer to empower your decision-making process. When faced with promises that seem too good to be true as you consider your next business investment, or even buying your next car, Your Fabulous Four serves as your secret weapon. Before investing in any educational programs, mentors, or most purchases, by using Your Fabulous Four, you can erase buyer's remorse and protect yourself from fraudulent claims. This tool doesn't just guide you – it steers you away from "shiny object syndrome."

These four steps, if you take the time to ask, will change your relationship with the internet, with content, and purchasing for the better. Who am I, in other words, the person you're learning from? Why do you care, and why can you trust me? One of the most important things I teach is to ask, "Why do you care?" or "Why does that matter?"

Creating Your Fabulous Four

Step 1: Who Are You and What Do You (or What Does Your Product) Do?

It seems like a super simple question, right? But if I had to guess I would estimate nearly 100% of businesses I have worked with spend too much time working on how to articulate what it is they do. Have you ever had a friend or loved one ask what your business does, and you feel like a deer in the headlights must feel? This feeling of fumbling your way through is what I call being stuck inside an Authentic Selling® Marketing Vortex. Many businesses will get stuck in an Authentic Selling® Marketing Vortex when trying to answer the first question in your Fabulous Four. The feeling or act of fumbling your way through to questions about what you do is an example of an Authentic Selling® Marketing Vortex.

Example: Who is Kendrick?

I'm Kendrick Shope, creator of Authentic Selling®, author, and media personality.

Marketing Vortex

Authentic Selling® Definition → Marketing Vortex: A state of continuously striving to achieve marketing goals without making significant progress, often characterized by repetitive efforts and strategies that don't yield desired results. In the marketing vortex, you can feel trapped in an endless cycle of planning, executing, and tweaking campaigns, with little to no tangible outcomes, making it challenging to break free and move forward.

Remember I said that often a business will get stuck in a marketing vortex when trying to answer this question? To avoid the marketing vortex, I've created some questions to help break down the "what do you do" question to help you get an answer you feel proud to share. These tools are tools within a tool to help you drill down in this case to more specific language. We call these tools Authentic Selling® Drill Down.

You can use these tool as you complete Step 1 of Your Fabulous Four or only if you get stuck when creating Your Fabulous Four.

1. Authentic Selling® Drill Down

   I _____.

   Which really means I _____.

   Which really means I _____.

   Example

   I teach businesses how to sell with integrity.

   Which really means I teach businesses how to make more money and reach more people.

   Which really means I help people/businesses create more freedom so they can do anything they want.

2. Authentic Selling® Drill Down

   People buy my product/service or hire me to help them _____.

   So they can _____.

   Example

   People buy my product/service or hire me to help them increase their sales and to find and close more customers so they can sell without being a bully, help more people, and make more money.

3. Authentic Selling® Drill Down

   Our customers often struggle with/experience _____.

   [Insert name of business/product] provides them with _____.

   So they can_____.

   Example

   Our customers often experience a decrease in sales. Authentic Selling® provides solutions to increase sales that work in today's fast-paced online world replacing outdated, pushy tactics. So their business reverses the decrease in sales and creates increased revenue and reaches more prospects.

Back to Your Fabulous Four.

Step 2: What's Cool About You?

But there's more to you than your Authentic Selling® Drill Down, right? I know you may be thinking this is a useless question but, said with love, you're wrong. Your customers want to do business with people they actually like so while my 25 years of sales experience is relevant, we need to share more. In today's social media online world, lifestyle and who you are outside of work is just as important as your expertise and experience. Consider what part of your personal life you are comfortable sharing publicly. The goal is for your potential customers to see commonalities between themselves and you.

Example: What is cool about Kendrick? (I commonly share at least part of the response below as an answer to this question.)

Like you, I wear a lot of hats everyday. I'm a daughter, sister, CEO, wife, and mom to the best kid on the planet who is my whole world. I was born and raised in Sweetwater, Tennessee, and am a third-generation graduate from the University of Tennessee. But here's something you may not know about me: I'm actively having an affair . . . with the greatest city in the world! I fell head over heels for NYC decades ago, and it will always be part of who I am!

I'm loyal to the core – and, believe it or not, I fell in love for the first time at 13. My very first crush? Jason Bruce, who was 18 and graduating high school while I was in 7th grade! So yeah, minor snag . . . he had no idea I existed! After Jason unknowingly shattered my heart – and, you know, because the whole thing was illegal – I rebounded fast. Enter Joe McIntyre from NKOTB. Joe was only four years older, not five, but still technically illegal! I fell hard, and here I am, 30+ years later, still a proud Blockhead and even consider Jason a good friend, you know now that he can't get arrested for talking to me and all that.

By now, you're probably catching on – I do things in a big way, am loyal to a fault, and don't take too kindly to following rules that cramp my style! A total mess of contradictions, you might find me in Neyland Stadium watching the Vols play on Saturday night or in NYC at a Broadway show holding the Red Bucket for my fave charity Broadway Cares Equity Fights AIDS (BCEFA)! As you can see, sharing what's unique about you helps potential clients connect with you on a more personal level. They get a glimpse of what makes you, you, and are more likely to remember you.

Step 3: Why Can Your Prospect Trust You?

Step 3 is your chance to share why you're the best at what you do. It's where you highlight your achievements, awards, and the success you've helped others achieve. It's a way to brag about yourself without sounding arrogant. By sharing these accomplishments, you show potential clients that they can trust you because you've got the experience and a proven track record of delivering results.

Example: Why can your potential customer trust you?

I have studied sales for more than 25 years, half my life, and was a top-performing sales expert for three Fortune 500 companies. I graduated top in my class from two corporate sales schools. I have been voted the #1 sales expert for health coaches, copywriters, and online business owners to follow as well as the top sales expert in the state of Arkansas.

Step 4: Why Does It Matter?

The final question in Your Fabulous Four is perhaps the most important. If you are around me for any amount of time, you will hear me ask this question. What you are basically trying to get across is what do the previous four questions and answers do for your potential customers and clients?

Authentic Selling® Pro Tip → Said with love, people – including your prospects and customers – don't care about you, they care about themselves and what you can do for them.

As you think about your answer to this final question, really consider what will change for your prospect as a result of working with you or buying your product.

Example:

Through Authentic Selling® I'm known for getting best-in-class results with clients and have helped businesses all over the world find more customers, close more customers, make more money, and create the freedom to do more of what they love. I will teach you to sell in a way that feels like helping rather than being a sales bully, which means more money in your bank account. The dictionary definition of selling is: "The exchange of money for a product or service." Translation, without sales your business is broke.

Putting Your Fabulous Four Together

Authentic Selling® Pro Tip → You will not likely use all of this at one time but it provides you with a structure you can use over and over to avoid fumbling your way through a very important question that often serves as a potential customer's first impression of you, your products, and your business.

Now you just combine all the steps into one series of paragraphs.

Example

I'm Kendrick Shope, creator of Authentic Selling®, author, and media personality.

Like you, I wear a lot of hats every day. I am a daughter, sister, wife, and mom to the best kid on the planet who is my whole world. I was born and raised in Sweetwater, Tennessee, and am a third-generation graduate from the University of Tennessee, but I am in a for-real love affair with NYC.

I'm incredibly loyal to the point I fell in love at 13 with Joe McIntyre from New Kids On the Block and am a Blockhead to this day. A total mess of contradictions, you might find me in Neyland Stadium watching the Vols play on Saturday night or in NYC at a Broadway show holding the Red Bucket for my fave charity Broadway Cares Equity Fights AIDS (BCEFA)!

I have studied sales for more than 25 years, half my life, and was a top-performing sales expert for three Fortune 500 companies. I graduated top in my class from two corporate sales schools. I have been voted the #1 sales expert for health coaches, copywriters, and online business owners to follow as well as the top sales expert in the state of Arkansas.

Through Authentic Selling® I'm known for getting best-in-class results with clients and have helped businesses all over the world find more customers, close more customers, make more money, and create the freedom to do more of what they love. I will teach you to sell in a way that feels like helping rather than being a sales bully, which means more money in your bank account. The dictionary definition of selling is: "The exchange of money for a product or service." Translation, without sales your business is broke.

Where to Use Your Fabulous Four

Your Fabulous Four consists of four simple steps that can be used in two ways.

As the seller, you can use your answers or a portion of your answers:

- At the beginning of a speech
- At the beginning of a webinar
- On social media
- Writing your bios

As the buyer, you should look for the answers to these questions when considering a purchase to ensure that your investments pay off and you can trust the business selling the product.

Shope Sales Stories

You bought this book because you want results. You want to turn your marketing efforts into paying customers. That's awesome for both of us because I'm here for all of that. The techniques you are about to learn brought me from a clueless college grad stumbling from job to job to being the #1 sales rep for major pharmaceutical companies to my spot as the CEO of my own million-dollar baby. These techniques have worked for thousands of students in every line of work you can imagine.

In fact, when I was a child not only did I want to be the greatest of all time in *something* but I believed with my whole darn self that I was going to change the entire world.

Whether my dream was to be a singer (I can't carry a tune), ice skater (I grew up in the South), actress (still know every line in *Rocky III*), or that month when I was four years old and I wanted to be a sex dancer (I snuck downstairs and saw a few minutes of *Flashdance*), I went all in. Whatever my THING was at any given moment I could always come up with creative ways to practice. Even though I lived in the tiny, rural town of Sweetwater, Tennessee, I was convinced that I would be a superstar. I'm sure some of the adults in my life thought of me as deranged – but looking back, I decided to call myself ambitious. After all, my parents always told me that I could do anything if I worked hard enough and put my "mind to it." For better or worse, I believed I could do *anything*.

By the time I went to college though, my "plans" to make it big and change the world seemed like a childhood fantasy. I had matured, grown up, and thought I had to start behaving like an adult. While my friends embraced college and wilded out a bit, I started to shrink. Within a couple of days I had lost all my confidence . . . and my ability to figure out how to get to the Humanities building on the big University of Tennessee campus in Knoxville on my own.

Here's the thing, y'all. When you start to lose your confidence, even a fraction of it, the whole shebang is gone before you know it and you're done, finished, it's over until you can find it again. I started to do what I see some of my clients doing when they come to me: spin out. I continued to have less and less faith in my abilities to do anything. I even started beating myself up for believing in myself! I thought things like, "Who are you to be famous? Just do what everybody else is doing and be happy with a business degree." I felt angry because I *did* want to be like my friends – interviewing for entry-level positions in marketing or advertising or finance, landing their very first jobs and feeling full of excitement about the future. I was mad because the only things I had ever really wanted to do – acting, singing, dancing, changing the world – seemed impossible and implausible.

Somehow over time I had lost touch with everything that made me . . . me.

I knew I had to figure it out so I went to the career services office and started taking all kinds of tests. But the results? You guessed it: actress, entertainer. But I didn't think those paths were possible for me, so I assumed I was screwed. I ended up graduating with a psychology degree. Over the next six years, I had four different jobs. I even went back to school . . . for two weeks. But in that time, I also realized I was better than most of my colleagues at talking with people, doing customer service, and selling. I assumed those things would be baked into what I was "supposed" to do. So I ended up as a telemarketer, signing people up for credit cards. But pretty quickly into that job, I realized their "offers" were exploitation in disguise so I quit. I ended up selling lumber, which is where I learned a key to sales is believing in what your product can do for people. You have no idea how excited I could get about a piece of plywood. But pretty soon I got tired of talking about screws, so I decided to take a chance and apply to work at GlaxoSmithKline or Eli Lilly as a sales representative. I have no idea how I landed the interview, much less two job offers, without knowing someone at those companies, but I did.

Working in pharma was a fun job that afforded me the opportunity to travel, shop, and have some flexibility. Pharma was good to me. I made life-long friends and learned tons of priceless skills. Along the way, I got married to my husband, Blake, and we had a daughter, Halianna. My confidence began to come back and a small glimmer of the girl I used to be who wanted to do big things came back, too. I was excellent at pharma sales, made a lot of money, and had a lot of freedom within the scope of my job. But something still felt off.

I remember a particular night like it was yesterday.

I was sitting in a pink rocking chair, rocking back and forth holding my newborn daughter. Looking at Halianna, I knew that little piece of heaven, that being right there in my arms could do anything, be anything she wanted. This little baby – my baby! – had unlimited potential. I wanted her to believe in herself as much as I did when I was a kid. I wanted to nurture her the way my parents had. So every night I rocked her to sleep. That's right. I said *every night* I rocked her to sleep. None of that putting her in the crib. I wanted to hold her. I wanted to smell her. I wanted to fill her full of positive energy, hope, and possibility. I wanted her to believe she could do anything before she even knew what any of those words meant. And that one night, the idea hit me like a ton of bricks, like a leg of lamb, like my credit card statement. Decades ago, my momma and daddy held me just like this. They breathed all those same limitless possibilities into my stream of consciousness. There's not a doubt in my mind, even to this day, that my mom believes I can do anything. (I don't know about my dad. He's a realist.)

But what had I become? A dancer? Nope.

A singer? Definitely not.

A professional, Olympic-caliber ice skater? ARE. YOU. KIDDING. ME.

There wasn't even a rink in my hometown. Even though being an actress was kinda realistic – Reese Witherspoon grew up a few hours away from me – I hadn't been in a single play since I was 16. Clearly, I had let everybody down. Or was I just living in the real world?

Because giving up childhood dreams felt responsible to me. It might to you, too. It's what most people do. Everybody in my life at the time had given up their wild and crazy dreams for a "safe" career, a money-making career, a home for their spouse and children. But sitting in that rocking chair night after night, the idea of being okay with the status quo began to feel unacceptable, almost nauseating. I think that little four-year-old girl inside of me was giving her last best effort, her one last fight to wake me up.

She was screaming. She was singing Bon Jovi at the top of her lungs. I had come so far from that little girl who believed she could change the world. I didn't even know that girl anymore because I had been living in "reality" for so long. However, I knew that I wanted to be the mom who walked the talk instead of just giving lip service to a dream.

In the past, I had heard athletic coaches say, "I'll never ask anything of my players that I can't do myself." And in my game of life – that moment was IT. The bottom of the ninth with the score tied. I had to swing the bat, go big or go home. I was either going to put the ball in play . . . or I was going to play it safe.

Right then. Right there. Sitting in the nursery I made a choice that changed my life. I wasn't too old, or too dumb, or too anything. Throughout this book you're going to have the opportunity to read the conclusion of this Shope Sales Story and dozens of others because this book is about more than selling. I chose to become the woman, the mother that my daughter could look at and say, "My mommy did it. She believed in her dreams. She sacrificed. She worked. And she achieved what she wanted." We had a fine life before this night. But fine just wasn't good enough. Not for my husband who loved me, not for my parents who had believed in me, and not for myself. And settling for a life that was less than I wanted wasn't even close to good enough for my daughter.

Picture this. Over the years, your wife has excitedly announced dozens of cockamamie, half-baked, wackadoodle, head-in-the-clouds schemes. One night this crazy gal bounds into your bedroom, right before you are asleep, excited as all get out and announces, dramatically:

"I'm living a lie."

Bless him, Blake simply said, "Okay. Tell me more." And I proceeded to share my awakening. I tell Halianna that she can be anything she wants. Right now she doesn't understand that, but one day she will. And she'll ask, 'Hey mom, did you want to sell drugs for a living?' (Obviously, the legal kind.)

"And I'll have to tell her no, I gave up on my dream. But you should follow yours – it'll be that whole do-as-I-say-not-as-I-do thing. And I can't do that." I went on to explain that I didn't want our daughter Halianna to look for role models at school or on TV or God forbid, on social media. I told my husband that *I* wanted to be the most important role model in our daughter's life.

At the time, I'm sure my poor husband was thinking, "Oh God. This business is her next *thing*." And to be fair, I understand. At one point, I was sending videos, unsolicited, to Oprah! I had tried out to be an NFL cheerleader even though I had zero dance experience and had only cheered for Sweetwater High. All of my "things" up until that point had been total disasters.

But behind every one of those wild ideas was an insatiable thirst to find IT. Ever since I was a little girl, I had been on a quest to find my one big dream. What I was meant to do in this world. Every time I thought I found "IT" I went all in. And this time I was different.

Six months later, I quit my six-figure job and started an unproven online business.

Sound familiar? This was IT, y'all!

I hired an executive coach who had me read a Martha Beck book. Briefly, my thing was becoming a life coach. But I'm not so great at allowing people to find their own way. Instead of leading people to drink the water, I hold a gigantic bottle to their lips and MAKE them drink. Life coaching clearly wasn't IT for me. Still searching, I joined a business mastermind. Another entrepreneur in the group mentioned that she was having trouble closing clients on sales calls. I figured that with all my experience and success in selling, I could help.

After 90 minutes, my new business bestie said "This is what you're supposed to be doing." I remember telling her that I didn't even know what I did, exactly. But lucky for me, she had written down everything I said. Her notes became the early version of Authentic Selling® 10 years ago. And honestly? Maybe I shouldn't have been surprised. At that point, I had been a top performer in sales for multiple Fortune 500 companies. I was one of those people who could sell water in the middle of a flood. IT had been right in front of me the entire time – but I had dismissed my talent like I had dismissed my dreams.

Since then, I've taught Authentic Selling® to more than 1,500 people and created millions in revenue for myself and others. I am the greatest of all time at teaching sales to online entrepreneurs and coaches. And guess what? My job includes getting to sing, dance, and entertain *every single day*. (I'm sure I could figure out how to ice skate *and* teach sales at the same time, but . . . there's still not a rink in Knoxville that will let me.) In fact, during the pandemic I got to meet my biggest celebrity crush over Zoom.

Yep, I got to meet . . . Joey McIntyre from New Kids On the Block! I am a huge New Kids fan and do not hide it. And though my love of music – especially NKOTB – has helped me close some sales from fellow music fans, my business – my IT – has become wildly successful because of two things: Belief and Selling.

We already talked about selling so let's talk about belief for a second. Back in college, I took a children's literature class mostly because my friends (education majors) were taking it. But that class ended up changing my life, because it's where I got to read *The Polar Express* for the first time. Keep in mind, this was *years* before the book was made into a movie.

But when I read that book, I had a spiritual experience.

The Polar Express is magical. Though I can't do the work of author Chris Van Allsburg justice in a quick summary, the plot is about a boy who doesn't believe in Christmas and Santa Claus. Through an otherworldly experience on a train that runs to the North Pole, the boy realizes that both Santa and Christmas are real. He ends up with a bell from one of Santa's reindeer as a gift to remind him that magic is everywhere. And though he can hear the bell ring for years (and so can his sister), the adults in his life can't hear it because they don't believe in Santa and the magic of Christmas anymore.

The end of *The Polar Express* describes how everyone in the boy's life, including his sister, gradually stops being able to hear the bell ring. The very last line of the book is:

Though I've grown old, the bell still rings for me, as it does for all who truly believe.

To say that I am changed by this book would be a huge understatement. (Huge.) Not only was that children's lit class my absolute favorite of all the classes I took, but I also wrote multiple papers about *The Polar Express* for other classes. When everyone else was writing about Socrates in Intro to Philosophy, I was writing about Santa.

Belief is at the center of everything I do.

It's how I show up in life and what I bring to every encounter, every relationship . . . everything. At the end of each video in the Authentic Selling®

University digital library, I say, "I believe in you and I believe in your business" and that's not a throwaway line for me. It's not bullshit. Because the magic that exists when you believe is core to so many things in life, from happiness and success to selling.

You might have heard the saying: *If you don't believe in what you're selling, then you're not going to be able to sell it.* And while that's not entirely 100% true – there are some gross salespeople who only care about making money – believing in your product or service and truly understanding how it benefits your clients and customers makes a difference. Think of it this way – would you rather talk about something you are passionate about, or something that bores you to tears?

Back when I sold lumber, I wasn't very successful at first. I found it really hard to get excited about hurricane brackets, plywood, screws, and nails. Until I realized that I was selling someone a way to secure their home in a storm. Or build the house of their dreams. Or to create the raised planter beds a spouse wanted in the backyard. When I started to tell myself stories about what these boring-as-hell products would do for my customers, my results were amazing.

Belief will do more for you than just help you sell. It's what will keep you going when you are crying on your bathroom floor because you got fired for not meeting your sales target, or when the 10th person in a row who booked a discovery call tells you they can't afford your services. Or when your spouse or mom or bestie questions what you're doing. That's when belief is crucial.

As salespeople, we believe that we are meant to do something different with our lives. We believe at a core level that we can change lives and make an impact with our work. Starting a business isn't for the faint of heart. It takes a lot of guts and a lot of courage to put yourself out there, to quit a job, to funnel money into something that has no guarantee of pay off. Or even to be vulnerable and honest enough to grab this book.

But at the same time, it's so easy to lose our belief in ourselves. When clients first come to me, there's often a gap in their belief between what they say they want and what is actually happening in their lives and businesses.

But here's what you need to know: I'm a country gal from East Tennessee who had to go through a review board to get into college because my ACT score was too low. (I had good grades but . . . standardized tests are not my friend.)

If I can do this, anyone can. I believe that and if you don't, that's okay. If you can't believe fully in yourself right now, that you're going to close 8 or 9 out of every 10 sales you try to make by implementing the strategies in this book, I can do it energetically for you.

But what I'm asking you to do in the meantime is to keep going.

When you end up crying in the bathroom, when someone doubts you, when that potential client says no, hear my drawl saying "I believe." Here's the truth: I believe in you, even if you don't – yet.

And if you're meant to be successful at this business you've got going, then you will be successful. And if you're not, well then that's okay, too.

I trust you'll make the right choice.

Before we move on, though, I want to make an essential point. Running a successful business isn't what you see on social media, hear about in free webinars, or read posted in Facebook groups. It's not sitting on a beach watching cash roll in *or* working your ass off every single day. Instead, in the past 10 years of being an entrepreneur myself and helping others, I have seen that you need three things for a successful business: grit, grace, and gratitude.

Grit to grow your business.

Grace to forgive your mistakes.

Gratitude for what you get and how you learn and who helps you get there.

And you need all three of those components to sell effectively, too. In this book, I'm going to give those tools and a ton of awesome, simple techniques that will help you get more clients, make more money, and have the freedom to do what you love.

Chapter 1

Your Authentic Selling® Mindset

Authentic Selling® Quote: "Selling is helping."

– Kendrick Shope

Authentic Selling® Gems from Chapter 1

- ❖ You will learn how to use your Authentic Selling® Sales Guardrail and avoid feeling icky, sleazy, slimy, or gross when selling and asking for what you want more of from life.
- ❖ Uncover the five foundations of Authentic Selling® so that you can use them to guide you to close more sales.

The first thing you need to know about selling is this:

Selling is helping.

But before I tell you more about that, let me tell you how I got here.

When I was little – and no, I'm not telling you my whole story or what year I was born – but when I was just five freaking years old, I thought I could change the world. I didn't really know what "changing the world" meant, by the way.

One day, my aunt asked what I wanted to be when I grew up. Little did she know, that innocent question ignited a fire in me that still burns today. I was prancing around in a white dress and sunglasses, and I said with full conviction, "I'm going to change the world!" When she asked how, I replied, "I'm going to be an entertainer."

From that point, I was on a mission to figure out what kind of entertainer I would become. One night, instead of sleeping like I was supposed to, I laid awake pondering, "How will I change the world? How will I help people?" That's when I heard music and thought, "What's that?"

Like a real pro, I army-crawled out of bed, not wanting Dad to catch me. Peeking around the corner, I saw our fancy new Curtis Mathis VCR – those were a big deal back then – and my parents watching *Flashdance*. If you haven't seen it, the movie is about Alex, a talented woman with no formal dance training, who dreams of being a professional dancer. She works as a welder in a steel mill each day and as a cabaret dancer at night. Alex is doing what it takes to make her seemingly impossible dream of auditioning, being accepted, and affording the tuition at an expensive and prestigious dance school.

My five-year-old brain didn't grasp any of those nuances. All I saw was Jennifer Beals, the star, fierce in her leg warmers dancing across the stage. The next day at school, I proudly declared, "I want to be a sex dancer!" That went over terribly in my small Bible Belt town and before the end of the day my mom got called to the principal's office.

Turns out, being a "sex dancer" wasn't my true calling to change the world, but everybody thought I'd be the next Madonna back then so I was sure it would work out.

Soon after, my aunt – it always happened at her house – gave me a book where kids went around asking, "Am I this or that?" Like, "Do I sing like a beautiful bird or an unholy goat?"

I'm not sure how I planned to be both a sex dancer and Madonna, but I'd prance around holding my hairbrush mic, fully committed to the dream of helping others through performance. I even prayed nightly, "Please let me be Madonna. I'll help everyone who needs it."

At seven years old, I asked my dad the fateful question: "Do I sing like a bird or a goat?" You can see where this is going. He joked, "Oh baby, you really do sing like a goat." I was crushed. "Dad, you don't mean that! I get all the parts in church plays!"

But those careless words stuck with me, even more than 40 years later. People say words don't matter, but oh, they matter so much. At that point, I was convinced – I wouldn't be a singer *or* dancer and that meant at seven years old, I began making choices that steered me away from my true calling.

2
Authentic Selling

Maybe I could be an actor instead? See – this passion for performing still sticks with me today. I usually take the stage wearing my Valentino patent leather shoes with bows on them – as it turns out, Beyonce has the same shoes. I didn't buy them because of her, but how badass is that? They have this big, bold bow that I love. Valentino, bring back the bows and enough with the studs already!

Anyway, the minute my fabulous feet hit that dusty backstage floor, I'm transported. You can see the dust floating in the lights and smell that distinct backstage scent that's unmistakable no matter where you are. And I just fall in love with performing all over again, no matter what I'm doing, as long as I'm on that stage.

From there, I decided with certainty – I would be an actor. I was so serious about it that I recorded all of Rocky III and IV using my prized Jambox from being the top cookie seller at school. Starting with Rocky III, I'd get decked out playing Adrienne, acting out full scenes like I was in a luxurious bathrobe opposite Sylvester Stallone himself.

I could probably still quote those movies word-for-word today. Someone challenged me on that in New York once, and after I started reciting it, they quickly admitted defeat: "Okay, I'm out. You're right, I was wrong." So I kept practicing and practicing.

By then I knew for sure – I wanted to be a performer. It was my happy place, my calling. I was meant to change the world through performing, though I had no clue how. I grew up in an East Tennessee town, in one of the poorest counties in the state, with no opportunities for acting, singing, dancing, you name it – unless it was at church.

But something inside me insisted that's what I was born to do, like how a kid just knows they'll play in the NFL someday. The path was uncertain, but the dream burned bright. With humor, grit, and a deep love for entertaining others, this small-town kid was determined to make it big.

The Five Foundations of Authentic Selling®

Speaking of football, y'all, I'm from the South, and any Southerner knows football is a religion down here. I can remember – true story – when I told my dad I was getting married, he said, "Well honey, that's fine, but don't plan your wedding during duck season or UT football season." We won't go into what duck season is here, but my Southern roots are important because I bring some of that southern hospitality into Authentic Selling®.

You know, there are lots of things that make Authentic Selling® unique, and one of them is that I created it from the ground up. I got to pour into it the things that I knew made me successful after selling for more than a decade as a top-performing sales rep.

And one of those things is being thankful. It's gratitude.

You'll notice that almost every sales tool you learn from me, because Authentic Selling® has tactical, practical, tangible sales tools that anybody can use, most or many of those tools start with gratitude. They start with a genuine "thank you."

And that is so important – starting with the genuine thank you, starting with gratitude, is the number one foundation.

The foundation is what the whole business was built on.

When I don't know an answer, when I'm confused, when I'm unsure of a decision, I look back at the Authentic Selling® Foundations. It's sort of like the 10 Commandments of selling, but there are only 5.

Authentic Selling® Foundation #1
Start with a genuine thank you.

There's incredible data and research about gratitude. But in selling, just so you understand this, most of the time, people who are getting ready to be sold to, they know they're about to be sold to, are a little anxious. This has actually been studied – you can see it. And they're expecting us, as the person selling to them, to be icky, sleazy, slimy.

So start with a genuine "thank you," like: "Hey, thanks for showing up here today. I genuinely appreciate it and respect your time. I know we're all busy, so just genuinely, thank you for the opportunity to speak with you today." Then you ease that anxiety.

Not fake, not gross, just a thank you. You put the buyer's mind at ease, and already they trust you just a little bit more, all by saying thank you, all by starting with a genuine thank you. That's why it's the First Foundation of Authentic Selling®.

Have you ever been to a live show? I love Broadway, how at the end, the actors and actresses come out, they take their bow, and they're so happy and full of gratitude. You know, they go to the orchestra pit and point to the musicians. Even at my daughter's high school, they do this. Like, we're so full of gratitude for the people who helped make this come together.

And it reminds me of being a performer myself and the immense gratitude I feel every time I step onto that stage, and the immense gratitude I feel when I step off after a performance. I was at my daughter's school not long ago, helping with their musical, and I was the only one on the stage. And I had this thought – I could stand on this stage, full of gratitude for the kids getting ready to perform, for hours, just because it's such a magical experience.

So that starting with a genuine thank you reminds me of just how I felt – so full of gratitude – when I had the chance to be on a stage. And that gratitude onstage has stuck with me my whole life.

I was so sure I was going to be a performer.

So How Did I Land a Sales Job?

Well, that's a great question, and the truth is sometimes you just need a job! But I was always good at selling. I mean, selling is kind of like you've got a little mini-stage and mini-audience anyway, if you think about it, so I had fun with it.

I'd always won the top sales prizes in my school – the bake sales, the cheer squad, the St. Jude fundraisers. I remember my Granddaddy saying, "Kendrick, you got such a great personality, you need to be in sales." And I would be like, "No, I'm going to change the world. I'm going to be an entertainer."

But when I graduated college, I had to get a real job. I had to start paying some bills – anybody ever been there before? And I got a telemarketing job . . . which I loathed but I was thankful to have. I thought it would be easy and I'd be doing what I'd always done when I did fundraisers for the school.

See, I'd never had an icky, sleazy, slimy, or gross approach when I was selling anything. Now, of course, we've all had those cringe-worthy experiences where the person across the desk from us is being disgusting, but I didn't sell like that.

I loved selling, but for some reason, this new telemarketing job made me want to crawl under a desk and hide. It still, to this day, makes me shiver. It took me a while to understand why.

I just couldn't stand it. I loved it, but I hated it. And I realized what was going on. This was back in the day when finance companies were doing high-interest mortgage loans (the government has since shut those down because they were such a scam, y'all – a legit scam).

But these well-known companies would hire people who knew nothing about financing and knew nothing about accounting but were good salespeople. And we would try to get people to convert their loans – you know, like when you buy a mattress on a same-as-cash finance deal and get 0% for six months? A bank buys that loan and finances it. And in the process, they get your credit. With the credit check, your name ends up on a list somewhere and so then you get telemarketed:

> "Hello, Mrs. Person! I see you have three credit cards. We can put that all on one credit card for you for one low monthly payment."

That's what we were doing. And initially, I thought we were helping people get out of debt.

There was this woman who is still one of my all-time favorite customers ever. I met her during this job. Sweetest woman you'll ever meet. I can still see her face. We did a mortgage loan for her. And she said to me: "Miss Kendrick" – that's what she called me – "Miss Kendrick, I just don't want it to be revolving."

And so I went to my boss and said, "I'm just making sure this is not going to be a revolving loan, that it's not going to keep growing, because it's a big concern for her." And he said, "It's a mortgage loan, Kendrick. It's a mortgage loan."

Well, that seemed to answer that for me.

So we did the mortgage loan. I felt so good about helping this woman I adored and her husband. But about three months later, she came in with her coupon book and said, "Hey Miss Kendrick, why is my balance going up? I've been making all my payments."

I looked at it, puzzled. "Well, that shouldn't be the case." So I pulled her paperwork, and at that moment, I suddenly understood the different *types* of mortgage loans. When my boss said it was a "mortgage loan," we had actually done a second revolving line of credit on her house.

My stomach turned.

I didn't know it then, but this would later become the Second Foundation of Authentic Selling®.

Authentic Selling® Foundation #2

We tell people this is the Golden Rule, the thing you cannot break:

Selling should never feel icky, sleazy, slimy, or gross.

If it does, you're doing it wrong.

I had looked this sweet woman in the eye and assured her, "No, that's not what we're doing." But I was ignorant because my boss told me it wasn't a revolving line of credit. So I said, "Miss [name changed], we're going to fix this."

I told my boss, "We have to turn this into an installment loan, no questions asked. That's what I promised her. It's the ethical thing to do." We eventually converted it to an installment loan. But the day she and her husband signed those papers, ensuring their debt wouldn't revolve anymore, I quit on the spot.

I've never done that before – quit without notice. But I couldn't do it one more day. I felt personally icky, sleazy, slimy, gross. Two years later, the federal government shut down this kind of predatory lending saying, "You can't do this to people. It's unethical."

For the first time, something I had been good at and enjoyed – my little mini-stage – showed its dark side. They say everything has shadow and light; I saw the shadow. I realized people out there are doing this to consumers.

The older I've gotten, the more I know you have to advocate for yourself. And as a businessperson, you've got to remember your customer is a human being, too.

Authentic Selling® Foundation #3
Believe in the life-changing difference your product or service makes.

I didn't believe in my job anymore, but fortunately, I was able to learn this with my next job, though it took me a while. My next job was selling lumber, and that is as ironic as it sounds for those who know me. I'm not a construction kinda girl, y'all. I literally wore a hard hat with Valentino boots. I was supposed to wear steel-toed shoes, but I just wouldn't.

Still made my sales quotas, though!

And I learned some incredibly valuable lessons when I worked at the lumber company, Georgia Pacific.

The first thing was that it was impossible for me to sell lumber because I didn't *believe* in lumber. That sounds wacky, but I didn't know what lumber *did*. And because I didn't know what it did, I didn't care. If Louboutins were made out of lumber, it might've come sooner to me, but they aren't, and so I ended up having to go to Lowe's one Saturday and flagging down one of the people in the lumber department.

I ran up to him in my heels and said, "Tell me *everything* about lumber."

Holy Valentino, did that change things for me. I learned all about lumber that day from that incredibly patient man, who humored me for nearly an hour, telling me all about how OSB board protects windows during a hurricane, what kind of lumber is used to frame houses, how it could even be used for framing beautiful art or whittled into instruments.

And then, all of a sudden, I liked lumber.

Lumber saves lives. Lumber builds houses. Lumber may be boring but it makes nearly *everyone's* life better.

And after that, I could talk to my customers about it because I believed in it. The lesson from this is you have to believe not just in yourself, but also in the life-changing difference that your product or service makes . . . or it's going to be incredibly hard to sell it.

I don't care if you're selling water, Diet Coke, Sarah Happ lip gloss, Taylor Swift tickets, or medicine. You have to believe and know the *difference* it makes, or you can't sell it.

Authentic Selling® Foundation #4
Create a raving fan with every interaction, but don't be a doormat.

There are different ways you can create a raving fan with every interaction. Still, one of my favorite ways is to have an incredible product.

Doesn't sound like rocket science, does it?

There's a place in Oak Ridge, Tennessee, called Big Ed's Pizza. If you haven't been, you're missing something. Now Big Ed's is not known for its ambiance. They literally serve you pizza on a paper plate so small, your pizza hangs off napkins – paper napkins that break if you try to eat your pizza with them.

But it's the best pizza you will get **anywhere**. And it doesn't matter if it is zero degrees or 99°; you will find a line outside of Big Ed's Pizza waiting to get in because it is consistently delicious. And so they create raving fans.

Authentic Selling® Math illustrates the overall effect of creating a raving fan with every interaction. If you're going to "create a raving fan" you need to know how and why you're investing the extra effort to make this happen. There are five great ways to do this:

1. **Consistently having a product that exceeds expectations.** In the simplest terms, this means that you don't have many returns because your customers are happy with what they've bought from you.

2. **Delivering the best customer service possible.** According to HubSpot, "93% of customers are likely to make repeat purchases with companies who offer excellent customer service." And not only that, they're willing to pay more for a brand that provides a great customer experience.

3. **My personal fave is doing the common things uncommonly well.** This means picking out one thing in your day-to-day interaction with customers and asking yourself, "How can we surprise and

delight them? How can we do this better than anybody else?" Everyone sends a newsletter, but how can *your* newsletter be done uncommonly well? We'll be talking more about this later.

4. **Making your buyer feel surprised and delighted.** Customer experience goes beyond sending them a quick response if they email you or picking up the phone if they call you. It's about going above and beyond to make them feel like you treasure every penny they spend with you – loyalty programs, early access, VIP special editions – all these are proven to increase your lifetime customer value (LTV) from a customer.

5. **Routinely treating your customer like more than a number or dollar sign.** A great example here is Disney Cruises – everyone on the cruise gets a gift every single night they're on the ship, the staff knows your name, and you walk the red carpet and get announced when you board the ship. Disney takes "Be our guest," very seriously.

Customers *want* to be your raving fans – you've just got to give them a reason to be!

As Henry Ford said, "Quality means doing it right when no one is looking."

But the key when creating your raving fans is to remember not to be a doormat at the same time. There's a saying in customer service that "the customer's always right."

The customer is not always right.

Many times, the customer is wrong. So there are times when you have to lovingly redirect, times when you can't do what the customer wants – like give away a car for free.

Ask yourself, "How can I create a raving fan in this situation while avoiding being a doormat?"

Authentic Selling® Foundation #5
Follow-up is a MUST.

Research shows the number one reason people – you, me, anyone – do not buy from anywhere, whether Best Buy, Apple, or anywhere else, is lack of trust. We don't trust that the product or service will deliver what the person says it will. So how do you trust someone?

Trust is a big deal, right?

One of the easiest ways is to follow up regularly on a consistent schedule. Because lack of trust is overcome by consistency. Consistency equals trust, trust equals buyers. Doing something as simple as learning to follow up can double your business, statistics show.

Here's an example. Another great thing working at Georgia Pacific gave me was meeting a man named Ed Caraway. Ed has already forgotten more sales techniques and strategies than I will ever learn. The first time I met Ed, I was in eastern North Carolina, staying at a Holiday Inn, and I was still in my early twenties.

Ed said, "Now listen, I'm going to pick you up tomorrow morning at 6:00 a.m., not 6:01, not 5:59. And we're going to go to XYZ Lumber [name changed] and see the buyer. Now, the other thing you need to know is I smoke, and I'm not going to roll down the windows. And I don't want you to say anything more to these customers that I've called on for 40 years other than 'Hello.' Just smile and look pretty."

Now that's a lot to take in, right, as a brand-new salesperson on a new job? But I'm so thankful I followed Ed's lead because he taught me how to be an *excellent* salesperson. He taught me the meaning of "create a raving fan with every interaction."

He did that by leading by example. Every Monday morning at 6 a.m., we'd show up at XYZ Lumber and we'd have a boberry biscuit with the buyer. He didn't look at us as salespeople; he looked at us as friends.

So much so that I extrapolated what we did at Georgia Pacific to make us the number one territory, and brought it to my next two pharmaceutical jobs. My cardiologists knew I would be there on Mondays with treats for Marvelous Monday. My neurologists knew I'd be there on Tuesdays for Terrific Tuesday. I said I was coming, and I came right on time every single week. I was so consistent that when I went on vacation, they would call me, saying, "Kendrick, where are you? Everything okay?"

And when medical offices were shutting pharmaceutical reps out due to government regulations, I was considered part of the office staff, not a rep anymore, and I *still got in the door*. Because I went in each week with the goal of creating raving fans with every interaction and I was consistent in my follow up.

Your Sales Guardrail

Selling should never feel icky, sleazy, slimy, or gross, right? But just because I say so doesn't mean it never will. So I created a tool, and this little tool is often people's favorite thing they learn with Authentic Selling®.

It's called your Sales Guardrail, and I bet you didn't even know you had one. But you do – everybody does.

The Sales Guardrail is basically your barometer or thermometer to keep you from going over into slimy grossness. On the right side, we've got that stereotypical pushy way of selling. On the left, we've got the "if you build it, they will come" passive approach – or "if they're meant to buy, they'll find me." Neither one works – neither uber-pushy nor uber-passive.

But as we get closer to the middle, to your Sales Guardrail, there are varying selling styles that will work. This is what makes Authentic Selling® magical – the ability to move up and down the guardrail, a sliding scale. One person reading this may be comfortable asking questions that feel more aggressive to others. That's okay, as long as you're not crossing your Sales Guardrail – that line of being too pushy or too passive.

You want to communicate as close to that Sales Guardrail as possible without going over into pushiness or slipping into passivity. If you're being too passive, you're not getting enough customers. What's really cool is you can use this tool in other areas of life too, to see if you're making the right decision – something you'll see later on that I wish I'd done in my own life!

So what makes this really magical is people's guardrails are different, and Authentic Selling® gives you the freedom to say, "I'm not comfortable with that follow-up approach. Instead, I'm going to do this."

It doesn't force you to do something that pushes you over your guardrail. It allows you to find another way to create the same outcome while ensuring selling feels like helping, not bullying.

Authentic Selling® Tools Takeaways

Selling is helping. So if it doesn't feel like you're helping customers, pause and ask: How can I make this feel more like helping? Right there, you've used two key Authentic Selling® principles – your Sales Guardrail and our North Star of "Selling is helping."

You also learned the **Five Authentic Selling® Foundations**:

- **#1: Start with a genuine thank you.** Why wouldn't you?
- **#2: Selling must never feel icky, sleazy, slimy, or gross.** If it does, stop and find another way. It's the Golden Rule of Authentic Selling®.
- **#3: Believe in the life-changing difference your product/service makes.** If you don't, you'll struggle to sell it.
- **#4: Create raving fans with every interaction, but don't be a doormat.** Research shows these "soft skills" separate money-making businesses.
- **#5: Follow-up is a must.** It's proven to double businesses. So if constant follow-ups would feel icky for you, let's find an approach that doesn't.

Your **Sales Guardrail** separates Authentic Selling® because it's not "my way or the highway." It allows you to slide up or down comfortably. Other programs might say, "You didn't do this right, so bye!" But with your guardrail, there's always a helping way that works within *your* personal boundaries.

Chapter 2

Your Customer's Money

Authentic Selling® Quote: "Your customer's money is none of your business."

– Kendrick Shope

Authentic Selling® Gems from Chapter 2

- ❖ You will learn why the most important sale you will ever make is to yourself.
- ❖ It's not about money . . . no really it's not.
- ❖ People pay for what they value.

The Most Important Sale You Will Ever Make

I'm going to take you through an exercise that – warning – might make you feel icky, sleazy, slimy, or gross. But it's a great opportunity to grow as a leader. Before we jump in, just know that I am never ever ever ever ever going to ask you to use this tool with a customer. Never ever. Picture Taylor Swift in her pajamas, looking into the camera and saying, *Like, ever*.

Sales trainings other than Authentic Selling® might use this technique with customers, but we don't. This exercise is simply a way to flex your Authentic Selling® muscle and skills as a leader. So how do you know if you believe? You need to know the answer to this question:

Why should someone go into debt to buy your product or service?

Yep. You just found out why my friends say I'm sweet as pie but tough as nails.

I know there are two dirty words in that question: Should and debt. But it's not relevant what you think of those words. If you believe in your product or service, you know the answer to that question. Remember, you never have to share with a potential customer why they should go into debt to pay for your services. But to succeed at Authentic Selling® (and selling in general) you need to know the answer for yourself.

I know the answer for this book. I know how radically the advice in these chapters is going to change your life. I also strongly believe in spending money to make money. So, the money you spent on this book is going to be well worth it. It's the best decision you've made in a while, in fact. Even if you put it on a high-interest credit card or went to a payday loan shop to get the cash, I feel confident you made a solid choice because you will earn that money back – with interest.

Here's a hint: When you can answer the "debt" question as passionately as me, then you are sold on your own products and services. And you've mastered one of the five Authentic Selling® foundations in this chapter: Belief; which is awesome because I believe in you and your business. I believe it is never too late to follow your dreams. I believe that your message deserves to be heard. And in case you aren't sold yet, I'm ready to give you the tools to help you share your message, impact the world, and make some money. These foundations will help you get there.

And when you doubt, just remember – I believe in you and I believe in your business.

Don't Get Thrown Out of the Office

One of the things you'll inevitably hear if you've been selling for more than a couple of months is, "You're not really selling until you get thrown out of an office." Now, obviously that applies to face-to-face selling. In telemarketing, it'd be "until you get hung up on," although that's much easier.

There's this old-school thinking that selling must be confrontational – that you're not making a difference or getting to "yes" until you cause some friction, confrontation, uncomfortableness. I remember the first time I heard that. I was in my first pharmaceutical sales job, and up until then, my whole life, I'd been sure I wanted a job where I could genuinely make a difference and feel that impact.

Now, I know some readers might be anti-modern Western medicine, and that's okay. This book isn't trying to convert you either way. But I was a drug rep – I sold drugs, the legal kind. I was a pharmaceutical sales rep, so some examples will relate to my decade in that field. If you're triggered by legal drug sales, just view the stories as illustrations for the tools. I'm not trying to argue one side or the other.

At that point, I really believed I was making a difference. I'm a firm believer in modern medicine, the human body's wonders, how it works, and learning about its mechanics. And I was damn good at my job. I took a territory ranked last in the nation at #425 and made it #1. Every one of my main products ended up #1 nationally during my pharmaceutical tenure.

Part of what made me such a great sales rep was what I learned from Ed Caraway about consistency. But the other key was my phenomenal partners who understood the drugs' science inside-out, like my former RN rep partner. That allowed me to be the emotional voice – sharing stories of how these medicines changed lives. We made a fantastic team representing our hometown, Knoxville, Tennessee (Go Vols!), down in Atlanta. I loved it.

Then I got too comfortable. There came a time when a manager told me that classic line: "You're not really selling, not making a difference, unless you're getting thrown out of offices." I'll never forget looking at him, thinking he probably wanted to fire me right then, and saying, "My mama didn't raise me to get thrown out of offices." They'd just invested six figures sending me to corporate sales training, where I graduated in the top of my class. And here I was, giving this manager lip, basically refusing to be that disruptive salesperson.

The Authentic Selling® Approach to Selling

My approach was completely different. You earned the right to be there. Remember Ed Caraway telling me, "Don't say a word, just turn around and look pretty. I'll tell you when to talk." It sounds sexist, I know, like I was hurting womanhood everywhere. But here's the thing: I was earning the right to be there because those men in eastern North Carolina weren't going to trust me, an outsider, to talk about lumber. They worked very differently.

I thought the same about my doctors' offices. When you graduate pharmaceutical sales training, you get all these marketing materials with 90-second, 30-second, even 5-second pitches – which is ridiculous, by the way, because doctors are fast-paced. You're supposed to launch into these canned product details. But if I was the doctor, I'd be thinking, "Who are you to waltz in here and tell me, someone with extensive medical training, what to prescribe?"

Now, in fairness, there are reasons reps do that. But optics matter – how it looks and comes across. So I decided against that approach. The first time meeting each doctor, I simply shook their hand, put my Southern accent and bright red hair on full display, handed them my business card, and said, "I'm Kendrick, your new pharmaceutical rep, and I'm going to be unlike any rep you've ever met. I hope you have a good day."

My manager hated it because it wasn't the company script I was supposed to follow by diving into the sales pitch. We got out to the car after that first day, and he said, "Kendrick, you can't sell that way." I replied, "Okay, here's the experiment. I told you I'm not getting thrown out of offices. Give me a quarter. When offices start shutting reps out, which we all know is coming, I'll be the one still getting in."

It was almost like a wager – not between me and him, but between me and my job. If my approach didn't work, I'd probably lose my job. That's how strongly I believed in earning the right to be there, not just bowling people over with a pitch. And sure enough, it didn't take 90 days; in about 60, as offices started closing their doors to reps, I kept getting invited back because I'd earned being part of that office culture.

Your Right to Sell

I didn't jump straight to telling doctors a thousand things they already knew. Instead, I led with questions. Yes, "Questions are a salesperson's best friend." But what does that mean? Am I supposed to walk in and just rapid-fire, "Hey, how are you doing, what's up, how's it going?"

No, every call, every face-to-face interaction with a physician had one goal: for me to learn something I didn't know.

Learn One New Thing That Moves the Sale Forward

Notice what I did not say. I didn't say your goal every call is to get a "yes," that every time you see the doctor, you must get them to write more of your product. No, I said the goal is for you, the rep, to learn something. That means asking questions and truly listening.

For example, I might ask, "Dr. Holly, I'm obviously new to your office. When you see a type 2 diabetic patient who's failed on Metformin, what do you do?" Then, Dr. Holly answers. Now, you don't just pounce with, "Okay, great, we've got the answer. Let's sell aggressively!" That's a surefire way to get kicked out, which we'll cover more in "Steps to a Sales Conversation That Converts."

What I want you to see is that when people teach selling, they often don't go through the actual process. They just say, "Question, sell, listen." Okay, but what questions? In your sales calls, especially face-to-face, your goal is to learn something new that moves the sale forward. In pharmaceuticals, that means understanding the doctors' customers (their patients). What are they currently doing for them? Are they seeing this problem? This is where you uncover the pain points of the doctor's patients and the office itself.

It's arrogant to think you can sell to someone when you have no clue what they're struggling with. I see this all the time in the online world: "Listen, I've been doing this longer than you've been alive. Come on, have some brains, people." The same principle applies in face-to-face selling.

Sure, you can talk about the benefits of Drug A versus Drug B, but they may not even see those types of patients. Don't make yourself look uneducated or foolish. Instead, use a little tool I like to call the KISS method. In my head, I sing it like, "Pretty Woman, keep it super simple now." In sales, they say "Keep it simple, stupid," but I hate that. No need for name-calling, alright? I talk about the KISS method more in Chapter 8 when writing sales copy. But it also works when selling face-to-face.

The Old Way of Selling vs. the Authentic Selling® Way

Now you know there's an old way of selling that teaches confrontation and getting kicked out of offices to make traction. It advocates verbally vomiting as much information as possible about your product or service. Think about it from your perspective. How do you want to be sold to?

You might be thinking, "Well, I don't want to be sold to at all." Okay, great, but that's not what I asked. How do you want to be sold to? Do you want people rapidly firing off every single thing their product can allegedly do? "This beach waver can blah, blah, blah, blah . . ." Again, keep it super simple.

Do you want an altercation with salespeople? Why does confrontational selling even work? Because when you challenge someone's beliefs and prove them wrong, it can be effective. You might get thrown out, but then the person does their research, or you follow up with evidence showing you were right.

But here's the real truth: Confrontation sells because it works on people born male. Women have verbal processing centers on both sides of the brain; men do not. Due to evolution, women fear being ostracized from the group because in nature, a female cast out often equals death. Men don't have that innate fear.

In the animal kingdom, males fight for dominance and mating rights. When men sell through confrontation, it triggers the release of oxytocin, serotonin, and sex hormones in the brain – some of the same chemicals involved in sexual arousal. So, sure, they enjoy selling through confrontation. I hate it.

This approach worked for a long time because men were the primary salespeople, and their targets were mostly other men. It functions well in male-to-male interactions, but not so much male-to-female, regardless of who's selling or being sold to. Now, I'm not saying confrontation should never happen. The Authentic Selling® foundation of "Create a raving fan, but don't be a doormat" still applies. Sometimes confrontation is necessary, especially if someone is behaving inappropriately.

But it shouldn't be a premeditated sales tool, like planning on having a chest-thumping match to get thrown out and then magically become best friends. That's so inauthentic and won't work for many of you. For some, it might, and if you want to learn confrontational tactics, go for it – just not from me. It's not my style.

I prefer quality conversations that move the sale forward. Every time you enter an office, your mission is to learn something new that advances the sale.

It's Not About the Money

I don't know if y'all knew this about me, but I can literally predict the future. I know it sounds a little presumptuous, but I can predict the future because I know this to be true: It happens to every single person who sells.

I try to avoid absolutes like "always" or "never," but I'm telling you, this is as sure as my hair is red. At some point, more than once, someone you're selling to will utter the most dreaded words in sales, "I can't afford it."

Oh, it just feels awful to hear that, doesn't it? It makes your stomach squeeze, and you start thinking, "What am I supposed to do? I don't want these people to go into debt." You want to be someone who is different and who conducts business ethically. That's why your customer's money is none of your business.

But here's what you need to know about your customer's state of mind: They pay for what they value.

My crystal ball (that I don't need) says 100% of the time you will hear, "I can't afford it." There's a lot of psychology behind why we say this as buyers, as potential customers. You tell someone selling you a new iPhone, "I can't afford it," and they think, "Well, I'm not going to mess with them," or "Oh no, I don't want to convince them." It ventures into that icky, sleazy, slimy territory we need to avoid.

The way we sidestep that is by having this foresight, this not-really-a-crystal-ball, and knowing people will say they can't afford it no matter what. The hard reality for someone who's super empathetic, kind, and caring is this: It doesn't matter if the price is a dollar or $5 million. Nobody likes the price because they're working hard for their money.

It makes me think of that Donna Summer song "She Works Hard for the Money." (This is so much better when you can actually hear me singing it, by the way. Y'all, audiobook!) But truly, it doesn't matter if it's a buck or five mil. Nobody likes the price.

I don't want to give you my money. I've worked hard for it. I do want to take a trip to New York City, the greatest city in the world, to see Broadway. I don't want to hand over my cash. But I pay for what I value. I'll give you my money if I trust that you'll give me back something of equal or greater worth. People pay for what they value.

Caveat: Sometimes It's About the Money

Now, here's where you have to use a bit of common sense, a Sales Guardrail. If someone says to you – and this has happened to me before – "I'm trying to decide how to pay you and also pay my rent," that's serious. We need to be the bigger person here and say, "You know what? Selling is super important, but not as important as paying your rent."

In that case, it may be about the money, okay? So 25% of the time, it may indeed be about the money. If I were you, I'd be thinking, "What the heck, Kendrick? You just spent all this time telling me it's not about the money, and I'm starting to believe you. Then you turn around and say it is about the money? What gives?"

Here's the thing: This is why your guardrail is so important. This is why value trumps money, always. In the case of a woman telling me she's trying to figure out how to pay her rent and also buy from me, her shelter is so much more important than paying me in that moment. She sees the value in both, obviously, but the value of one trumps money.

We're going to tie all this together at the end of the chapter, so stick with me. But remember: It's not about the money, it's not about the money, it's not about the money. Caveat: Sometimes, about 25% of the time, it is about the money. But it's always, always about the value.

People Pay for What They Value

So, there I was, my first day back at my pharmaceutical sales job after having a baby. But of course, I had to be extra. One thing you'll learn about me is that I'm loyal to a fault. Keep that in mind when I tell you that I fell in love with Joey McIntyre from New Kids On the Block at 13, and he's been part of my story ever since.

Why do you care? Well, remember the part about being extra? I had been on maternity leave for 32 weeks because I went into pre-term labor the very day New Kids On the Block announced their first-ever reunion tour in 2008. See? Loyal to a fault.

Now, back to my first day post-baby. I had been out for 32 weeks, and my first week back, I was scheduled to attend a national sales meeting in Miami. So, on the Friday before, I met my sales partner at a coffee shop to "catch up" after missing over half the year. How does one even catch up on that much work, by the way?

Anyway, I was deep in the throes of postpartum, and Halianna was screaming for hours each day. Picture the loudest baby you've ever heard, then multiply that by about 13 . . . for hours on end. Since I had been on bed rest and maternity leave for 32 weeks, I read every book I could get my hands on about how to be the best mama to this kid. If you're a mom, you know that most books tell you to head to the ER if your newborn cries for three hours straight. The problem? Halianna cried for six hours most days. I took her to the ER so often they eventually told me to stop coming.

But before they kicked us out, one night we met an old, past-his-prime doctor. He took one look at me and said the reason Halianna was crying so much was because I wasn't breastfeeding. I understand some of you have strong opinions on breastfeeding, which I respect, but I couldn't breastfeed. And even if I had chosen not to, that's my choice. Side note: Can we stop being so hard on new moms?

So, if you're keeping track: 16 weeks of bed rest, 16 weeks of maternity leave with a baby who cried at the top of her lungs for six hours a day, and then some arrogant doctor tells me I'm the reason my child is crying. Textbook postpartum.

Now, it was time to go back to work. I was headed to South Beach for a week, which sounds like a gift for a new mom – but I was about to shatter into a million pieces. While meeting my sales partner, I burst into tears and could not stop. So, I decided this "catch-up" meeting was not helpful and went home, hoping for a fresh start after the weekend.

On my way home, I realized I had my first coffee since becoming pregnant, and let me tell you, I needed a bathroom fast. Too much information? It gets better.

I fly into my garage in my company car and rush to burst into the house. My mom had come down from Sweetwater to help with Halianna, who she had finally gotten to sleep upstairs in our three-story home, with the "brown noise" machine working overtime. But when I try to get in, I realize all the doors are locked, and my keys are on the kitchen table. Meanwhile, I'm on the verge of bursting, both emotionally and bladder-wise.

I start banging on the door, ringing the doorbell, calling my mom's cell phone. My mom, who's feeling pretty proud of her role as the new grandmother, is upstairs, oblivious to my crisis. I have no options left. So, I sit down in my front yard, fully dressed, sobbing like I'm in a daytime drama. And, you guessed it, I peed all over myself.

Not even 20 seconds later, my mom opens the door and says, "Kendrick, what are you doing here?"

So, what does this have to do with you and selling? According to *Architectural Digest* in 2024, a new toilet costs about $350. Back in 2008 when this happened, I would have paid $5,000 for a toilet, or even an extra key to my house. And no, I couldn't actually afford a $5,000 toilet – I had been out of work for 32 weeks!

Let me hammer this home with another little story. When I was brand new in the online industry, a couple of interesting things happened with potential customers. One of my first seven clients hired me for consulting at a whopping $197. She said she was worried, unsure if she could afford it.

Now, my guardrail didn't tell me this was a case of the caveat, that it was truly about the money. It was only $197, and she was starting a new business with all these other projects she was spending on. So, since I was the boss, I lowered the price. Sometimes you don' have that choice, but I made it.

Within days, this same customer came to our coaching call, all excited to show me her brand-new website that she paid $13,000 for. Here's the deal: Shame on me, not her. She negotiated a better price. When she said she couldn't afford it, what she really meant was, "I'm going to pay for this $13,000 website, I'm going to do this and that." In that moment, it felt like she couldn't afford it. But if she had enough for a $13,000 website, she most likely could swing $197.

So, shame on me for lowering it. That was one of my first seven customers, and I learned my lesson: We don't lower the price. It's not easy to be firm because I have people I love and adore, and I'll want to cut them a deal. But I don't. At Authentic Selling®, we don't negotiate on price.

Because I'm the boss, I made it a rule in 2012. And it held true until 2015.

In 2015, I was selling a $25,000 consulting package. I got on the phone with a woman who was giving me all the silent closes and buying signals you'll learn about later. But when I told her the investment, she burst into tears on the Zoom call. Not just kind of crying – she was gasping for air, saying, "I have been saving to work with you. I'm so excited about this. I know I need this!"

It got to me, hit me right in the solar plexus. It didn't matter that the rule was no negotiating on price. What mattered was I wanted to feel better. I felt this woman really saw the value in what she was getting. So I negotiated a lower price.

A few months later, she needed to take a break from coaching because she went on a month-long retreat to the Maldives. Amazing for her, though I'm so jealous! And yet, I had negotiated on price.

People pay for what they value. They may say, "I can't afford it," but that really means two things:

1. I'm not convinced I can trust you to deliver all these magical things you promise.
   This is largely because of the world we live in. People are skeptical of selling in general. That's just our reality. Folks get scammed and lied to all the time, so that wariness isn't going away. Potential customers will worry they're making a bad investment.

   My husband is the worst at this. He can buy something he's wanted, and no matter if it's a dollar or $200 (we've never paid $5 million), he'll spend days, weeks, even months justifying that purchase. He gets physically ill over the investment – he's the worst!

People buy on emotion and justify with logic. "I can't afford it" really means either "I'm not sure I can trust you. You seem nice, but I've been scammed before" or "I don't trust myself. I've got shiny object syndrome. I've bought 4,000 sales classes, and I don't know, Kendrick, if I can trust you or me." So the first thing "I can't afford it" tells you is there's a trust problem.

2. There's a value disconnect.

If you hear a potential customer say they can't afford it, and it's a value issue, what does that mean? It means they're not sold on the product or service.

In the first reason, that they weren't sure they could trust you to deliver on what you promised, they weren't sold on you. With a value problem, maybe the product or service is missing something they're looking for. Maybe they want hours of free coaching, and you don't offer that. Or they need one-on-one coaching, and that's not part of your package.

A value problem either means the customer is seeking something you don't provide, or they're just not wowed by your offer. They're not in a hurry to go out and buy this thing. Let's dive a little deeper into that.

Understanding Your Customer's Money Mindset

We've established that your customer's money is none of your business, but here's a further truth: People pay for what they value. Period. Full stop. If they don't see the life-changing value in your product or service, they're not going to spend their hard-earned cash on it. And why should they?

Your job is to communicate the value of what you have to offer, which we'll dive into later. But right now, step two of understanding your customer's money is recognizing that people pay for what they value. In this case, it's not about money, even if they say it is.

We're kind of dipping our toe into how we'll talk about objections later because you're going to get 19 incredible tools for overcoming them.

But before you can use those tools, you have to understand your customer's money on three levels:

1. Your customer's money is not your business. Stay out of it. Do you want your cardiologist looking at the holes in your jeans, deciding you can't afford the best treatment, and giving you a lesser product? No, you don't.
2. People pay for what they value. They'll even pay more for something with all the features they want than take a deal and save money, even if they told you they couldn't afford it. Your job is to show people the value of what you're asking them to do.

    It doesn't matter if you're trying to get a kid to go to bed on time, eat their veggies, or brush their teeth (and I've heard moms say they've used this for all those things). Or if you're trying to get someone to pay five million bucks for your product or service. They have to see the value.

    It's why we have homes with entire guest rooms on the off chance someone might visit. It's why we have four TVs in our house. Do we really need more than one? No.

    It's why some homes have two ovens. Mine doesn't because I don't value cooking. I'm terrible at it. But some people do.
3. The third thing we have to talk about with your customer's money may be the hardest one: debt.

Why Would Someone Consider Going into Debt for Your Product or Service?

We know people pay for what they value. We've talked about how your customer's money is none of your business and how people buy on emotion and justify with logic. But what about you? Where do you fit into this equation?

One of the foundations of Authentic Selling® is belief. You have to believe in the life-changing, even life-saving difference your product makes, even if you're selling something as simple as lipstick. And I know some of you are thinking, "How does lipstick change someone's life?" That's the question.

There's an Authentic Selling® tool to help you communicate the value and importance of whatever you're selling. When you get the value and importance right, you don't have to worry as much about objections. When you nail the value, people see they need to act now. They won't haggle over a $197 offer because they value a $13,000 website more. When you articulate the value correctly, you eliminate so many objections.

With Authentic Selling®, we're not talking about pushing ketchup popsicles on people who don't want them. Zig Ziglar, whose books on tape I listened to as I drove from office to office, talks about "no need." If there's truly no need, move on to someone who does need what you offer. There are plenty of people who need your product or service. That's a little PSA.

Your one job is to be the expert on what you're selling, to be so incredibly sold on it that you see it as a disservice to the potential buyer if they don't make this investment. Think about that for a minute. It's a disservice if Kendrick doesn't buy this lipstick today, if you don't pick up a copy of *Authentic Selling®*, if you don't buy these roses. It's a disservice to your customer because you haven't communicated the value.

So how do we communicate that value? How do we become so sold on our products or services that we're able to do our job well? I'm going to teach you a tool from my sales training, something I've taught in Authentic Selling® University. And to be honest, it makes a lot of people uncomfortable.

I need you to read my lips: I am asking you to never, ever, ever use this tool when actually selling. I'm asking you to never say these words to a customer unless it genuinely feels appropriate within your guardrail, which for most of you, it won't. This is an exercise to get you thinking, not to turn you into Mr. or Mrs. Icky, Sleazy, Slimy, Gross Salesperson. It's just a tool.

Here's the question: If it's a disservice for someone not to buy your product or service today, if it's hurting them, what are the reasons they should . . . ooh, dirty word alert . . . consider going into debt to buy it? I know, it makes me a little queasy too. I'm right up against my guardrail here, y'all. But remember, we're not saying this to a customer. It's an exercise for you to think through.

Why do they need it now, Kendrick? "I don't believe in debt." Doesn't matter for this exercise. Why do they need your product or service so badly? What's it going to save them from? What's it going to do for them?

Take lipstick. How does it really change your world? Well, lipstick has a ton of psychological benefits, from boosting confidence to making you feel like your lips are more kissable. And how does having kissable lips help? There's science proving that kissing, even air kisses, releases happiness hormones like dopamine and serotonin. It literally makes you happier.

Imagine if everyone had more of those feel-good chemicals just from wearing lipstick and blowing kisses. Yes, it's silly, but my point is that it might be worth going into debt for – to be happier. Lipstick can also be formulated with peptides and hyaluronic acid for extra benefits.

When you dig a little deeper, you can find real value in even something like lipstick. Or let's look at high heels. Studies show women feel more confident in them. There's science – and this is worth memorizing – showing that women make more money and are perceived as more attractive by both men and women when wearing heels.

You may not like a world so focused on beauty, but this is the data. If I sold shoes, you bet I'd be talking about this. "Wait, you're telling me these heels can help me make more money? Sign me up!" It's a justification to spend more on shoes. We just got a raise, permission to invest in footwear.

You've got to dig deep here. Why should someone consider going into debt for your product or service? It's not just surface-level benefits, not just "the shoes will match her outfit for the wedding." It's all that other meaningful stuff.

If the question of why someone should go into debt for your offering makes you super uncomfortable, rephrase it. What's worth going into debt for, period? Is a home worth it? Happiness, health, medicine? What about following your dreams, feeling more confident, landing the job, sending your kid to an amazing summer camp where they have the time of their life? What about shoes or lipstick?

Insert your product into those questions. How does it improve someone's happiness or health? How does it change their world? When you can answer that, you can talk about your product or service's life-changing benefits. That's your job, because your customer's money is none of your

Your Customer's Money

business, because people pay for what they value, and your job is to show them that value.

Authentic Selling® Sales Tools Takeaways

1. **Your customer's money is none of your business.** As a seller, it's not your place to make judgments about a customer's financial situation or their ability to afford your product or service. Focus on communicating the value of your offering rather than worrying about their budget.

2. **People pay for what they value.** It's rarely about the money; it's about belief. Customers will invest in a product or service if they believe it will deliver the results you promise. They need to trust that your solution will work for their specific needs and circumstances.

3. **Why would someone go into debt for your product or service?** As the seller, you must be completely sold on the value of your offer. The "why should someone go into debt" exercise is designed to help you identify and articulate the true, life-changing value of what you're selling. When you understand and believe in the transformative power of your product or service, you can communicate that value to potential customers with authenticity and conviction. I have faith in you and your business to deliver real, meaningful value to your customers.

Chapter 3

Authentic Truths

Authentic Selling® Quote: "All things being equal friends buy from friends. All things being unequal friends buy from friends."
– Kendrick Shope

Authentic Selling® Gems from Chapter 3
- ❖ Four stages of your customer's journey.
- ❖ People buy off of emotion and justify with logic.

Relational selling isn't a new concept but building positive customer relationships authentically rather than an icky, sleazy, slimy, sales tactic is.

Why It Matters

Authentic Selling® Truth→ Lack of trust, time, need are among the top objections you will experience when selling your products/services.

Authentic Selling® Math→ Sales research statistics teach us that people are more likely to spread the word via social media about a negative customer experience compared to a positive one.

Authentic Selling® Math→ Sales research statistics also teach us that nearly 80% of satisfied customers are happy to share about their positive experiences but businesses only ask them to share 11% of the time.

> *All things being equal, friends buy from friends.*

And

> *All things being unequal, friends buy from friends.*

Translation→ Customers are less likely to share objections that stop the sale and problems or complaints with your product/service.

And

Translation continued→ Customers are more likely to buy from your business, do repeat business with you, and share positive reviews with other potential customers.

Authentic Selling® Pro Tip→ Word of mouth is the best form of free advertising that exists and one of the most effective. Taking the time to invest in actually getting to know your potential customers means that you close more sales as well as repeat sales because customers enjoy doing business with you.

I hate the quote "the destination is the journey." I want to be at the destination. I don't even think that's the right quote, but you know the quote – where the beauty is in the actual journey, not in being at the destination. Yeah, forget that. I want to be at the destination, forget the journey. I always joke with my friends, "I've learned enough lessons, I'm ready to coast!" And you may be thinking, "Okay great, but what's this got to do with selling?" Well, we're going to get there. Trust the redhead, y'all.

You Think You Know Your Customer But You Might Not

Let me illustrate this with a more personal story.

My Husband's Stroke

Every time I share this story with students or clients, I am so humbled by the experience and people's reactions to this.

So, there I was in Chicago with a newborn-ish child, and I knew that I had to be better for her. I knew I wanted to be better for her. But that wasn't the first time this realization had hit me like a ton of bricks. Now, the realization may have sounded different – it wasn't necessarily "you need to be better for her," because, you know, she'd only been around for a couple of years. But the realization hit when my husband and I were first married.

We had been married for 13 months. I'm going to say that again for emphasis – 13 months. A year and a month, y'all. Not long, is my point. And it was a Sunday in June, and we were watching church on television. And with the snap of my fingers, Blake's speech became slurred. His face drooped to one side, he couldn't move one side of his body. And I had not yet worked in the healthcare field, but somehow I knew he was having a stroke. So I called 911 and said, "I think my husband's having a stroke." And the 911 operator said, "He's probably having a seizure, he's so young," because he was 27.

It's weird, because this moment as I remember it just comes sort of like flashes. When you're watching TV and the power goes on and off, and they're doing stuff for dramatic effect, you know – that's how I see this. So I called 911, the ambulance comes, Blake's on a stretcher in the ambulance. The ambulance driver said, "We think he has botulism." I don't know what botulism is. What are you talking about?

The Hospital

We get to the hospital, and I see my husband of 13 months lying there, unable to speak clearly. He could make noise but you couldn't understand a word he said, unable to move one side of his body, unable to walk. So, imagine, in an instant, going from perfectly healthy to not able to talk, walk, or write. He couldn't even write his name. And I'm thinking, "What in the world is happening?"

One of the first things I thought of was work. I need to let my boss know, and I need to let his boss know that he's probably not going to be in tomorrow, Monday. But I'm sure we'll be back in by Tuesday. That's what I thought.

I remember standing in the ER on my cell phone, calling Blake's boss and calling my boss. "I'm sure it's fine, but we're not going to be at work tomorrow." I remember calling my girlfriend and saying, "Hey, we rode in the ambulance, so when they dismiss him or release him or whatever, will you come pick us up?" And then I turned around and I saw the attending doctor on the phone. She had three or four textbooks sitting in her lap, on the desk in front of her. And I heard her say something to the effect of, "But he's only 27." And I realized, she's talking about my husband. All these textbooks and this phone call and all of this is for my husband. And we're at the place where they're supposed to know what's going on.

Having to Make a Difficult Decision

Then the neurologist shows up. And I've got to tell you, you know those people that you meet in life, and they just become these almost larger-than-life characters in your story? I've never seen this man again since we left Atlanta, but this doctor was like a cartoon character. He was so bizarrely unempathetic and out of touch with his emotions. He was a genius, but he comes in and he checks Blake out. And when he's done, he says to me, "Well, I think your husband's had a stroke. I can't promise you he'll live through the night, but what I can promise you is it's going to be a long ride, either way. So, you should go home and get some rest. Do you have family here?" Wait, what? What is happening? What?

And then the attending doctor walked up to me and she said, "Okay, we think that your 27-year-old husband – that you've been married to for 13 months" – she didn't say those two things, but just to reiterate the point – "has had a stroke. There are two types of strokes: ischemic and hemorrhagic. Ischemic means a blood clot, hemorrhagic means a brain bleed. If he's had a blood clot, an ischemic stroke, we can give him a drug called TPA. If you get TPA within the first three hours of a stroke, it can reverse all the effects. However, we need to do an MRI to confirm what type of stroke he's had. And we don't have time, because if we do an MRI, we're going to miss our three-hour window. And if we give him the drug and instead he's had a hemorrhagic stroke, a brain bleed, he will die. Not 'he may die' – he will die." And she wants a decision. Now.

You want to talk about pressure? We think that, you know, we don't want to put pressure on people when we're selling our stuff. It's like life or death. And in that moment, I felt so unqualified to make a decision for a man I had been married to for 13 months.

Making the Call

I am great in a crisis, most of the time, unless the crisis is mine. But anybody else's crisis, I'm great. I can hyper-focus, I am who you want around. I don't break down. I can isolate and say, "Here's what we need to do, let's go." Unless it's my crisis.

And so there I am, in ripped sweatpants, my shirt with stained food all over it because we were just lying around having a lazy Sunday. We'd been to the Cheesecake Factory for lunch. I had cried at the Cheesecake Factory because I hated my job, wanted to live my purpose – that was the most important thing in my life at lunch. And six hours later, I'm making a life-or-death decision for somebody I've been married to for 13 months.

So I looked at her and I said, "Look, I know that you likely are not able to answer this question. But I'm 26 years old. I didn't even know there were two types of strokes until you told me 30 seconds ago. If it's your husband or your wife or someone you love in there on that bed, what do you do?" I think what she proceeded to say was, "I can't answer that." And I interrupted her and said, "I'm not going to sue you. I'm not. I just don't know what to do. You've been through decades of school. You have the power to give me an informed decision here that I don't have the knowledge to make." And she said, "Give him the drug."

So I said, "I 100% made the decision on my own to give him the drug." And then it was a flurry of stuff happening. She ran off – form after form after form I needed to sign. "You may have just killed your husband." I mean, that was literally what I was signing. "What's his weight?" Because the drug was weight-based. I didn't know what my husband of 13 freaking months weighed, y'all. I mean, come on.

The Aftermath

And when all those forms were done, I called my mom and dad in Sweetwater, Tennessee. And I said, "Well, I've either just saved Blake's life or I've killed him." Matter of fact, no emotion. But I knew in that moment, we entered this hospital one way and we would leave completely changed people. I just hoped we both would leave.

The next four days were hell. But Blake got the drug within the three-hour window, and that saved his life. Any kind of issues, health complications that you have after a stroke, are called residuals. And he is basically residual-free. By the time his parents got there, he was laughing and joking. And it was a bizarre four days. And we were so lucky to leave the hospital together. And he walked out of the hospital. Not well, but he walked.

We had to go to the mall for the next few months and do old people walking, mall walking, you know. But I remember saying to him that day, it was such a juxtaposition or such a before-and-after moment for me. Because as I sat there at the Cheesecake Factory eating my meal and my brown bread that I love so much with butter, sobbing over a job that seemed so unimportant now. Life is so precious. I'm never going to forget that. I'm going to go and fill my days with what I love. And you're going to do the same. And we're going to take a trip every year, just for us. All these New Year's resolutions, right? I mean, really, we had just told the Grim Reaper to f*** off. So we're feeling pretty good about ourselves.

Lingering Impact

That good feeling didn't last, though. I was at the beginning of a customer journey. A lot of things changed. Blake got angry. Blake was mad that this happened. He's one of the healthiest people I know. And so he was livid when we finally figured out what caused it.

He had the stroke because he was trying to be healthy. He tore his medical vertebral artery, which just means an artery in his neck, when he was working out, lifting. But we didn't know he tore it. The clot broke off, tried to stop the bleeding, went to his brain. He had three strokes actually. You can see them on the MRI still to this day – his brain died. The first stroke was in his brain stem. And so we're very, very lucky.

But Blake was mad. And while I'm good in a pinch, in a chaotic situation, all that emotion has got to come out some way. And it does, when the threat of life or death isn't there anymore. And so rather than going back to work full of gratitude and full of each day as a gift, I went back full of anxiety, full of worry. "If I hadn't been there, what would have happened? Can I ever leave him alone again? What if he stays so angry? How do we make peace with this?"

Moving Forward

And I realized, the whole world moves on. You're there fighting for your life. And this sounds so ignorant, but if you've had a death in your family or a death of someone you love, you've probably experienced this – where you're so full of grief or so consumed with this moment, but you don't realize you turn the news on and you're like, "Oh, that election that I was so worried about happened. I didn't even know it." "Or that event that I was so excited to attend happened – didn't even know I missed it." Because you are consumed with being in the present of that moment, because you have no other place to be.

It would be seven years before I had Halliana and had that realization of "I have to be better for her." It took me more than a decade, y'all, to be able to act on that same bit of information, just presented a different way. The fragility and preciousness of life is a lesson I seem to need to keep relearning. But each time, I strive to carry that renewed perspective and gratitude forward, and to fill my days with more of what matters most.

What I would love to tell you is that having the awareness of how precious life is, and having a run-in that makes you realize how lucky you are to have each moment – or each 525,600 minutes like they say in *Rent* – only needs to happen once. But you and I both know that wouldn't be true. The majority of us know how lucky we are to just have another day. Yet, and I'm the world's worst at this y'all, I've been excellent at self-confession right here: I'm the world's worst. I get so bogged down by everything and so irritated, and can't see the beauty in the chaos or the beauty in the everyday.

Customer Journey Triangle

Why am I telling this story? Because it perfectly illustrates, in dramatic form, the concept of the customer journey. We're going to look at my story through the lens of that journey and see how you can apply these principles to your own life and sales process.

Yes, there's an overarching moral here: each day is a gift. But there are also highly practical, tangible things to take away, authentic selling tools. And the first is the authentic selling customer triangle.

This triangle is based on something I learned during a training for selling lumber at Georgia Pacific. I've since adapted it into my own authentic selling customer journey framework.

Let's walk through the stages of this customer journey. Picture it as a triangle. We all move through these phases, starting at the bottom with "unaware."

Unaware

In the customer journey, you begin unaware that a problem even exists. Just like Blake and me at the Cheesecake Factory that day we were unaware of his health issue; the problem was likely already there, we just hadn't experienced it yet.

Your potential customers are the same. They're going about life, and you, the expert, may see something that would improve their situation, but they're unaware of it.

It's like when you first learn in life coaching that you are not your thoughts. That negative self-talk – "you're a fake, a fraud, a failure" – isn't reality. Before that lightbulb moment though, you're unaware you're creating your own misery. Our customers start out unaware that they even have the issue our product or service solves.

Problem Aware

Next in the journey is "problem aware." I became acutely problem aware on the couch when Blake suddenly couldn't speak or move. It was scary in the moment, but almost comical in hindsight; we knew there was a problem, moving from unaware to aware.

Solution Aware

However, we didn't know the solution. Even the 911 operator and ambulance driver weren't sure – a stroke at his age? Botulism? Seizure? Different issues with very different solutions. We were stuck between being problem aware and solution aware.

This is crucial – it's hard to be solution aware if you're not problem aware. Imagine you're a book writing coach. Someone like me who's never written a book may naively think "I can figure it out" – problem unaware. Versus "I've tried and it's overwhelming, I need help!" – problem aware. Big difference.

As humans, we falsely believe we instantly know how to "adult." But just like walking, talking, and brushing your teeth, managing your mind is a skill you develop. Being a kick-ass salesperson doesn't automatically make you a great sales manager or teacher. Consuming info-products doesn't mean you know how to sell. No shame, but you need to identify the real problem before pursuing a solution.

Raving Fan

After unaware, problem aware, and solution aware comes raving fan; they've had a positive experience and will eagerly return as a customer.

Applying the Journey

Let's apply this. If you're using social media to sell and hearing crickets, your audience may be problem unaware. Posting about the benefits of a stroke drug makes no sense to healthy 26-year-olds like I was. It doesn't apply to their life.

Your content must engage the unaware, not just those who know they have a problem and are seeking a solution. It's a common pitfall; you need material that makes the unaware sit up and take notice.

Consider our real-life example. We went from "it's botulism!" to "it's a seizure!" to "it's a stroke!" I saw a problem, but didn't know what it was. Then I became solution aware. And often multiple solutions are needed, like TPA plus rehab for Blake. A complex problem.

Beware of any marketing claiming a single product is a panacea for everything. Even Vanilla Ice only promises to solve "a" problem, not "all your problems!" Know where your offer fits once people are solution aware.

Then there's the often-skipped step between solution aware and raving fan. A raving fan knows, likes, and trusts you. They want to buy everything you offer. How do you create raving fans? A key authentic selling principle: All things being equal, friends buy from friends. All things being unequal, friends buy from friends.

You don't have to be their bestie, but treating customers like a trusted friend is the best free marketing. The ER doctor advised me like a caring friend, even though we had just met. It made me feel safe in her hands, and our neurologist's, even if his bedside manner was gruff. He was a true expert on the brain, and that's who I turned to when my migraines later flared up.

Consistency breeds trust, which leads to buying. Being a genuine expert who cares for people consistently makes them feel safe and eager to purchase. It's a customer journey – unaware to problem aware to solution aware to raving fan. You need to pinpoint where your prospect is on that spectrum.

Raving fans are obvious; you've done business before. But the unaware are tougher to spot, since they're not engaging. When I asked 20,000 entrepreneurs if they needed a sales process to make money online, 100% said no! They were unaware they even had a sales problem, or that lack of sales was behind their money woes.

Why does this matter? Because selling, by definition, is exchanging money for a product or service. No selling, no income. And marketing, by the way, contains the word "selling!"

The Four Stages of the Customer Journey

So let's look at all four of these stages together.

1. **Unaware.** They're oblivious, they don't even realize they have a problem. They might be experiencing symptoms, but they haven't connected the dots yet.

2. **Problem Aware.** They're feeling the pain, the uneasiness, the dissatisfaction of the problem. But they either think it's just how life is, or they don't know how to fix it. When problem aware, they start exploring different solutions. Hiring a coach, reading a book, etc. It's like trying to get your kid to sleep; you might try bribery, wearing them out with activities, even empty threats. You're testing options.

3. **Solution Aware.** Two things happen here. One, you clearly identify the problem. And two, you know how to solve it. Going back to the bedtime example, you realize positive experiences are the answer, not threats. You've pinpointed the issue and the fix.

4. **Raving Fan.** This is the best free marketing ever. Raving fans tell everyone about you. They buy everything you sell. Why? Because you've consistently shown up, followed up, been kind and expert. You've built trust, which creates neural pathways in the brain. They're primed to buy from you again and again.

Selling Lumber

Let me illustrate with a less dramatic example than the stroke story. When I left the lumber industry for a job at Georgia Pacific, I was elated. Unaware I'd soon face dissatisfaction again, even though it was a great company.

I became unhappy because I wasn't doing what I was meant to do. I was problem aware and knew I needed a career change. The solution I zeroed in on? Pharmaceutical sales. The clothes, the flexibility, the chance to talk about the medicine that saved my husband; it seemed perfect. I'd arrived!

So I started interviewing, moving through the customer journey myself. First unaware I had a problem, crying to my husband at The Cheesecake Factory. Then problem aware, but unsure of the answer.

As I explored options for a psychology grad, I talked to relatives who worked in pharma. Bingo – there was my solution. I interviewed with two major companies. Here's the twist. Yes, I was going after the job. But they were also selling me on the company.

I chose the first one to make an offer, GSK. But the Eli Lilly rep, Stan Pinnerty, was a sales all-star. For three years he checked in. "Heard you're killing it in your territory!" "So-and-so said you won an award!" Not a hard sell to join Lilly, just friendly follow-up.

By the time I was ready for a change, Stan had made me a raving Lilly fan, without my ever working there. His consistent attention and clear leadership standards had me itching to join his team, all from one interview years prior.

See, if you create that "all things being equal" feeling for potential customers, when they have the money and timing, you'll be top of mind. You can pull a Vanilla Ice: "you've got a problem, I can solve it!"

But a word of caution. Becoming a raving fan can take time. There are ways to accelerate it, which we'll get into. But you've got to know where folks are in their journey.

Preaching the gospel of sales to 20,000 entrepreneurs who don't think they need it? Waste of breath. They're unaware of the need, so find ways to illuminate it. The hard truth is, this process demands patience and persistence. But the payoff of loyal, repeat customers is so worth it.

People Buy Off of Emotion and Justify with Logic

There's one more crucial thing to understand about the customer journey. People buy based on emotion and justify with logic. If you read nine sales books, at least seven will mention this. But what does it really mean?

It means you need a balance of emotional and logical appeals when discussing your product or service. Let me illustrate with an example.

If the doctor had come to me and said, "Well, Kendrick, this is the pharmacology of what TPA does. It goes through intravenously into the bloodstream and the CYP enzyme through the liver . . ." and a bunch of other jargon, I'd be lost. I mean, she'd be telling me how the drug works, but I wouldn't have the knowledge to grasp the logic.

What she did need to give me was enough logical product information to ask for help. Here's what she said:

> We're pretty sure we think your husband's had one of two kinds of stroke – a blood clot in the brain or a brain bleed. We don't have time to figure out which one it is, but there is this miracle drug called TPA. When people get that drug within three hours of a stroke, you can reverse all symptoms, can save his life. Problem is, we don't know, and if we give it to him and he's had the other kind, it'll kill him.

In the span of 20–30 seconds, she gave me a wealth of logical information I didn't have before:

1. They believed my husband had a stroke.
2. There are two types of stroke.
3. This is the type they think he had.
4. If they're right, there's a miracle drug available.
5. This is what the miracle drug does if they're right.
6. This is what the miracle drug does if they're wrong.

She went on to explain why they thought it was a clot versus a bleed, something to do with blood pressure. There were logical reasons behind their belief.

But what did the neurologist, the one with poor bedside manner, do? He skipped the logic and went straight for the emotional jugular with "I can't promise you your husband will live through the night." It doesn't get more emotional than that, does it?

I was already scared before hearing about TPA. My mindset had been "I'm calling people to come get us when we're discharged, sorry to inconvenience you." Then I was swiftly made aware, "Oh holy Valentino, you might be walking out of here alone. He may not leave."

That's the emotional part. The logical part is all the medical details the hospitalist shared about the drug. In that decisive moment, just like when your potential customers have to choose, it's emotion that gets them to enter their credit card, to say yes, to sign the contract.

But the minute I decided, I started justifying with logic. You know what else I did? I started calling people because I was worried, I needed reassurance. I phoned my parents and literally said, "Well, I could have just killed Blake." There's the emotional hook to get their attention. Then I laid out all the logical information.

My parents replied, "Baby, you did the right thing." Your customers do the same thing, even if the stakes aren't so dire. Here's a bonus tip: think about how you can help them reinforce that they've made a great decision after the purchase. Because you know their brain is going to want that justification.

Folks, thank you for allowing me to share this deeply personal story. When I told Blake it would be in the book, he said, "Well, you've already told it to 100,000 people, so I guess it won't matter." But I appreciate the space to share it in this way.

The Power of Stories

There's a reason I've spent so much time on this story. It perfectly encapsulates the key concepts we're discussing – the customer journey, and the interplay of emotion and logic in decision-making.

As you craft your own marketing and sales, think about how you can take your potential customers on a journey. Help them become problem aware, then solution aware. Paint a vivid picture of the pain they're experiencing and the relief your offer provides. Tap into those emotions.

But don't neglect the logic. Give them the features, the benefits, the reasons to believe. Enough to grasp onto as they justify their emotional choice.

The neurologist gave me the emotional push. The ER doctor provided logical reinforcement. Together, it was a powerful combination. That's what you're aiming for.

Not every story has to be so intense. Not every product is life-or-death. But the principles remain the same. Emotion gets them to act, logic helps them feel good about it after.

Master that balance and guide them on that journey from unaware to raving fan, and you'll have customers for life. Just like you, they'll be sharing their story of how you changed everything. And that's when you know you've made it.

Now, let's dive into how you can apply this in your business. It's time to put these concepts into practice and craft your own compelling customer journeys.

Authentic Selling® Sales Takeaways

Finding your customers starts with you. Before you can write sales copy or have sales conversations, you must know where your customer is on their journey. It all starts with what we covered in this chapter: you being sold on your own product or service. Once you believe, you can move forward.

1. **The Customer Journey:** Your customers will move through the Authentic Selling® Customer Journey:
   - **Unaware** – They don't know they have a problem.
   - **Problem Aware** – They feel pain or dissatisfaction, but may not know the solution.
   - **Solution Aware** – They're actively seeking answers, comparing options.
   - **Raving Fan** – They trust and want YOU, thanks to your consistent expertise and empathy.

   You must know how to communicate with customers at each stage, as the approach differs dramatically.

2. **All things being equal, friends buy from friends; all things being unequal, friends buy from friends.** The number one reason people don't buy is lack of trust. They don't believe the product will deliver, or that you're being honest. That's why the

raving fan stage is so crucial. When you consistently show up and deliver, you create trust; and trust equals sales. Remember: All things being equal, friends buy from friends; all things being unequal, friends buy from friends.

3. **People buy off of emotion and justify with logic.** Your challenge is to strike the right balance. Too much emotion and not enough logic can breed mistrust. Too much logic and not enough emotion can be boring and ineffective. Aim for a mix that engages feelings and provides rationale.

With these foundational principles in place, we're ready to dive into the nitty-gritty. Chapter 4 will explore your buyer's brain, and beyond that we'll arm you with hardcore (but not hardball) sales tools to guide people up the pyramid to yes.

Believe in yourself and your business. You've got this!

Chapter 4

Your Authentic Business

Authentic Selling® Quote: "Clarity comes from taking action."
– Jenny Shih

Authentic Selling® Gems from Chapter 4

◆ Be the expert.

◆ Avoid toxic marketing advice that keeps you stuck.

◆ Diagnose your customer.

I'm going to warn you, you will read tips in this chapter that are counterintuitive to what you've learned from other business experts. In the modern world of marketing and selling you will encounter a massive amount of toxic business growth tactics. Figuring out who your ideal client is and how best to serve them is a nonnegotiable when learning to sell. Unfortunately, too many experts teach that you need to know everything from your potential customer's shoe size to their blood type. This is some of the most harmful toxic business growth advice, leaving businesses stuck. Spending too much time getting to know your customer keeps businesses trying to identify demographics that do not matter. Even worse, many online business consultants use an "ideal customer avatar" exercise to shift the blame onto their clients when their consulting efforts fall short. Of course, understanding your prospect is beneficial to your sales process. This exercise becomes toxic when you ask so many questions that you never move past identifying marketing and sales language, but never begin the process of actually marketing and selling. Personally, I have no idea what my students and clients order at Starbucks. I don't care what they like to eat, I don't care what they like to drink, I don't care where they like to shop, I don't care how much money they make, and what they like to read. As an experienced salesperson, I can tell you that too much of this process is filler, busywork, or both.

Examples of Possible Toxic Customer Filler Avatar Work

- What they read
- How much education does your most perfect client have
- What's your client's order at the coffee shop
- Where your ideal customer lives
- What your customers do for fun

Instead of wasting time compiling useless information about your prospects, you can save time, create more persuasive social media, and advertising campaigns using Authentic Selling®.

Experts Sell More

Authentic Selling® Truth – your potential customer wants to buy from an expert. That doesn't mean you jump up and down with jazz hands telling everyone how brilliant you are. Instead, when you are a real expert, you are able to **show** rather than **tell** your prospects you're an expert through the language you choose to use in your sales process.

Let's say you're in the market for a new car. Do you want to purchase a car that is assembled by mechanical experts or are you okay letting your 16-year-old kid drive a car that was built by someone who has never assembled a car?

What if someone you love dearly was scheduled to have heart surgery tomorrow morning? Your two options for surgery are an expert medical surgeon who has successfully treated this specific condition thousands of times or someone who has only read a book about the heart and listened to one podcast about the anatomy of the heart. Which one of the two heart surgeon options would you choose? Using the car and heart examples, the reasons for buying from an expert seem obvious, right? You're not alone, your customers want to buy from an expert who understands their problems and the pros and cons of the available solutions. Like you, your customer doesn't want to sit around listening to a sales expert tell them how smart, experienced, and what an expert they are. Instead you can show your potential customers your brilliance and expertise using the Authentic Selling® Tools, Diagnosing Your Customer and Your Authentic Selling® Sales Map.

Authentic Selling® Pro Tip→ I use the word "diagnose" here loosely. (Also it doesn't matter what your personal opinion of antibiotics, pharmacology, or the health industry is because that's not relevant.) "Diagnosing" in this context is a tool for you to drill down to client language that shows your prospect that you've invested time to understand your client while showing your expertise.

Diagnosing Your Customers

Let's pretend my daughter, Halianna, woke up with a sore throat, a fever, and she's feeling sick to her stomach. Like any good momma, the first thing I do is whip out my phone. Not to Google – because then I'll be convinced she's dying of some rare disease – but to shine the flashlight on the back of her throat. And when I see those white spots back there, I instantly think: oh no, it's strep throat. So she's gotta go to the doctor, right?

When I arrive at the doctor's office, I will say something like "I think my daughter has strep throat." Our amazing pediatrician will likely ask me what symptoms Halianna has. When I tell her that she has a sore throat, is feeling sick to her stomach, and has been running a fever, the doctor will likely ask a nurse to do a rapid strep test.

After the test comes back positive – as I knew it would – the doctor will prescribe us antibiotics and ask us to come back in after the pills are finished to follow up. But here's what I want you to notice about this analogy. The doctor didn't prescribe antibiotics right away, did she? No. She needed to make sure the symptoms lined up with the actual pain points. And because the doctor took the time to verify that Halianna did actually have strep throat, the antibiotics will get effective results and we'll get to go on the Disney cruise we've been planning.

You might be wondering – what the heck does Halianna having strep have to do with my business? Everything, y'all. Sure as my hair is red, you can diagnose the symptoms and the pain that your customers are coming to you to resolve. Drawing the analogy further, think of your customers as Halianna and you're the doctor. It's your job to use the symptoms that your clients present to diagnose their pain points and offer a cure based on the results that your product or service achieves. You're going to use the information from Diagnosing Your Customers in the next chapter! Now that you've played "doctor" and diagnosed your customer, we're going to create your Authentic Selling® Sales Map.

Authentic Selling® Sales Map

Pain Points + Features = Benefits

Pain Points (What's showing up in your customers' lives before they work with you)

+ Features (Your product or offer)

= Benefits (Results after your potential customer buys from your business)

Authentic Selling® Definitions

Pain Point→ A symptom causing dissatisfaction in an area of your life or business. One of the ways I remember pain points is thinking of the TLC song "Creep." The chorus says "So I creep, just keep it on the downlow cause no one is supposed to know." Pain points are like that chorus, oftentimes your potential customer may be hiding ("keeping on the downlow") the fact they are experiencing them. Also, pain points can creep to impact other areas of your potential customer's life and other people in their lives. For example, if you are a business owner and having trouble converting customers, your family may feel the "creep" of the pain point because you're stressed and short tempered. 100% of consumers experience pain points. As we drill down into the pain points, we're getting clear about the discomfort customers are experiencing as a result of the pain point mentioned earlier.

Questions to Help You Identify Your Customers' Pain Points

1. What symptoms from the Diagnosing Your Customer exercise are showing up in the lives of your potential customers?
2. Describe the area of dissatisfaction in the lives of your customer that is driving your customer to seek a solution
3. How could/do these pain points creep?

Features→ A cure, solution, action that your potential customer can take to deal with the above pain points. Features are the "how" your product solves the problem your potential customers are looking to improve. The features of your offer consist of anything that is included in the solution you're selling to your prospective customers.

Questions to Help You Identify the Features of Your Offer

What is the action/cure?
Benefits→ What changes as a result of the features of your offer. Benefits are the transformation that is possible as a result of your offer. Features are "the how" you solve the problem, and benefits are the difference that your product or service makes in the lives of your customers and why it matters.

Questions to Help You Identify the Benefits of Your Offer

1. What changes as a result of the cure?
2. How does it change?

These tools will all come together to form an entire sales system; they're highly effective. Your Authentic Selling® Sales Map forms the foundation of everything you will learn in the remaining chapters. Right now, as we learn the first few steps, you may be feeling like, "I don't understand how this is going to make me millions of dollars or how this is going to help me close more sales or how this is going to, whatever."

And I get it. But you have to give the whole process a try. Your Authentic Selling® Sales Map can be applied to your sales pages, your sales conversations, your social media, your follow-up to help you close more sales. You can use the following Take-n-Tweak language to help you get started creating your own Authentic Selling® Sales Map.

Sales Map Language Take-n-Tweak from Chapter 4

Pain Points Take-n-Tweak

- What do you want to change about your circumstances and reality?
- Utter lack of joy
- Constantly undermining your best intentions – set a New Year's resolution but don't keep it?
- Vicious cycles of self-guilt
- Ridding yourself of behaviors that interrupt the life you dream about
- Finding yourself in the same ole place
- Everyone telling you how lucky you are, you have a wonderful family, and beautiful kids
- Your happiness is created outside of you
- Continuing to experience difficulties over and over
- You may be happy, but the real joy is missing
- Struggling to get unstuck
- Breaking the pattern of self-sabotage
- Your happiness is dependent on external factors

- Something isn't right
- Everything feels same ole same ole
- Something is missing
- Striving for more
- Striving to succeed
- Striving for excellence
- Stumbling on happiness instead of creating it
- **One-third** of people who suffer from depression are not helped by the standard treatment of pharmaceuticals and/or talk therapy
- Not all depression is the same
- Feeling of helpless and hopeless

Features Take-n-Tweak

- Coaching sessions
- Classes
- Video lessons
- Meditations
- Done for you assets
- Facebook group
- Book

Benefits Take-n-Tweak

- Imagine the fresh possibilities
- Self-audit what's not working and begin a journey toward your "best life"
- Life is good really good
- There is laughter in your life

- There is love in your life
- There is light and family
- There are long walks that feel like a fall afternoon
- Passion
- Perseverance
- The secret to _____
- Peak performance
- Personalized approach to _____
- Work smarter
- Live better
- Intervene in your own life and get more joy, meaning, purpose, etc.
- Invaluable guidance
- Change your life
- Healing depression
- A new way forward
- Whole person approach
- Lasting relief
- Find the missing puzzle pieces for your life. It could be the difference.
- Path to lasting joy
- How to negotiate a raise or contract
- Road map to making choices that help you live the life you want
- Simple tools you can use to get what you want
- Craft a persuasive message
- How to act boldly beyond your limits so that you're happier
- Take control of your career
- Alleviate allergies

- How to actually stick to new habits
- Turn your life around
- Real-world strategies for overcoming adversity
- Effective tips to increase your happiness
- Live your healthiest life
- Empower you to eat better
- Maximize your energy
- Become a better leader
- Tips to negotiate deals and contracts
- Get ahead in the workplace and life
- Fight cancer
- Dramatically improve your life
- Never slide backward again
- Develop a healthy lifestyle – no rigid dieting required
- Make choices that serve your desires
- Never feel I have to choke down healthy food again
- Live longer
- Make an unforgettable entrance
- Live cleaner
- Live happier
- Take control, prevent symptoms of illness
- Resources for all-around healthy living
- Relieve insomnia
- Skillfully communicate
- Get out of your own way
- Detox your environment
- The ultimate plan to health

- Lessen your risk for type 2 diabetes
- Balance your hormones including the stress hormone
- How to create glowing skin and mental clarity
- Replenish your mental, physical, and emotional energy
- Relieve headaches
- Expert recipes to help with skin disorders
- Simple, natural steps to feel better and healthier
- Steps to unlock your real motivation
- Better manage your time
- Put your professional future into your own hands
- Run more effective meetings
- Simple practical ways to eat healthy delicious food for life
- How to find your purpose and pursue your life's real work
- Discover your life's purpose
- Make willpower your secret weapon without becoming exhausted
- Inspiration to become who you're meant to be
- Practical help and inspiration to help you find the job you're meant to do
- Live a life that is connected, influential, and free
- Discover why you were placed on earth
- Do more than simply exist. Live.
- Honor your calling

Rocking Chair Epiphany

Some of our most intimate time as a mom and a daughter was when I would rock her to sleep at night. I'm a mom who rocked; I have no regrets about that. Loved putting that baby in my lap and rocking her to sleep. I started this tradition of telling her every night she can be what she wants to be in this world. It started with belief, and you may recall that it's a pretty big deal in my life.

One special night in Chicago, Illinois – that's where we lived; I was a drug salesman then, the legal kind – I was rocking Halianna to sleep, saying the same mantra, the same mantra that I had said for years: "You can be anything you want to in this world, but you know it all starts with belief." And that's when it hit me like a ton of bricks.

I realized that this child who I loved more than anything was going to look at me one day and say, "Mommy, did you want to sell drugs for a living?" And I was going to have to say, "No, I didn't. I wanted to be an actress. I wanted to perform. I wanted the stage." And then my child was going to have the realization that all this "you can be anything you want to be in this world" was just lip service. I mean, it didn't work for mom, so why would it work for her?

I put Halianna in her bed, in her beautiful crib, and I burst through the French double doors into our room in our Chicago apartment. I said to my husband (he was playing Madden football at the time; yes, I'm putting our kid to bed, he's playing Madden football), "Blake, you need to listen to me. I tell our child every night that she can be anything she wants to be in this world. All she has to do is start with belief. And one day, she's going to wake up and say, "Mommy, is this what you believed? Is this what you wanted?"

"So, I have to be a better person for her. I have to be a better example for her than somebody who gave up on their dreams, than somebody who is the most successful drug saleswoman on the planet but secretly cries herself to sleep because she's unhappy." And I said to Blake, "I'm quitting my job." And Blake said, "No, you're not." And I said, "Okay, well, hold on. Buckle your seatbelt, 'cause the ride's about to get bumpy." And oh boy, did it get bumpy.

"Clarity comes from taking action."

– Jenny Shih

You're going to hear a few stories throughout this book about a woman named Jenny Shih. Jenny is one of the most brilliant people I've met and I'm lucky to call her my friend. As lovely as friends are, why do you care? Because Jenny Shih has taught me some of the most impactful lessons of my life and it would feel out of integrity not to share them with you. The first of these gems is that "clarity comes from taking action." Another way of thinking about this is staying stuck or doing nothing is a choice and it's a miserable place to live. We put too much pressure on 18-year-olds to understand what they want to do with the rest of their lives, and not enough permission to change our minds as an adult. I feel like I've done all kinds of jobs, right? I mean, if you think back to some of the things that I have told you so far, there was Kendrick the exotic dancer. If you missed that chapter, you really should read this word for word. There was Kendrick the drug salesman, right? I mean, wow, this woman has had a life!

After that night of rocking Halianna to sleep and realizing I had to become a better version of myself for her, I took action almost immediately by hiring an executive coach who had me read *Finding Your Own Northstar* by Martha Beck. This book changed my life because I realized I could tap into wisdom that came from my body not my brain.

Authentic Selling® Confession→ Despite being the number one sales representative for my product at my pharmaceutical company, I looked in the mirror feeling like a failure, fake, and fraud . . . every single day.

Discovering life coaching and Martha Beck was life changing for me. I thought I had discovered my purpose. I became a Martha Beck–trained life coach and was going to help people discover that same awareness I had.

The $25,000 Mastermind

After the completion of life coach training, I realized life coaching had changed my life. But I was a terrible life coach. I wanted to tell people what to do, not lead them to discover it for themselves! I had just attended an event hosted by Marie Forleo called Rich Happy & Hot Live. I mean, who doesn't want to be rich, happy, and hot? Now if you don't know Marie Forleo, she's kind of like Oprah to online business. I mean, I joke and say she's like the godmama of online business, except she's very young. But at the time I didn't know who Marie was, and I wasn't there to hear Marie, see Marie, anything Marie. No disrespect to Marie, I would end up learning a mountain of information from her but at this point, I attended Rich Happy & Hot to hear one woman speak: Danielle LaPorte. By the end of this event, I had lived through Hurricane Sandy and joined a $25,000 business mastermind run by the one and only Marie Forleo. How I even ended up in this mastermind is a testament to selling, y'all. The people in this mastermind were extremely successful business owners. I'm talking about multi-million-dollar business owners or people who were just really crushing it. That's how this weekend event started off, right? By Saturday, I clearly knew who Marie Forleo was. I mean, she was an incredible source of knowledge to learn from, and I learned so much at that event. And I remember thinking at that event, my life is never going to be the same.

At the event, Marie pitched her mastermind. And I wasn't really a good candidate for said mastermind. But when she was done, I approached her. And I kind of grabbed her hand, which I know you're not supposed to do. She's on a stage and I'm eye-level. And she said, "I'm sorry, I have to go" or something.

And I said, "I know, I know, I know. But look at me. Remember this red hair. My name's Kendrick and I am meant to be in this mastermind. May not look like it on paper, but I know it." You want to talk about selling it? I mean, I'm sure Marie and Danielle LaPorte talked about this person who they were worried about. Might have been a little bit dangerous, who's crying and calling Danielle Jesus, and then I'm grabbing Marie's hand. But Marie looked at me eye to eye, and she said, "Okay." And if you know anything about Marie, what I can tell you is the woman gets her stuff done.

So I applied for Marie's mastermind. At the time, I did not have any idea how momentous this experience would be. I turned my application in on Sunday to one of Marie's right-hand people, who I'm still friendly with to this day. And I followed up with the same message, "It may not look like it on paper, but I am meant to be in this mastermind." Well, now, first of all, that's some dang fine selling, y'all. It's a $25,000 mastermind, and I'm the potential customer and yet, I'm the one telling people how much I need to be in it. Like I said, that's some good selling!

Why This Matters to You

Running a business is challenging. If anyone tells you otherwise, run away from them as fast as you can because, as sure as my hair is red, they're not giving you the full story. It's not rocket science to understand that when starting a new project, your confidence may be shaky. Before you can sell anything to anyone, you need systems in place to recognize and overcome these shaky moments.

My journey involved many wrong turns and detours, like selling lumber, selling drugs, attending business masterminds for life coaching, and even becoming a life coach. All these experiences eventually led me to start the right business. As Jenny Shih says, "Clarity comes from taking action."

It would be nice if we could give ourselves a little grace, realizing that we're not born knowing how to run a business. Just as we're not born knowing how to sing, play the piano, or ride a bicycle – unless we're prodigies – we learn these things. Unfortunately, we often don't learn to be patient with ourselves or to give ourselves room for mistakes. We learn that falling off the bike and getting back on isn't easy; it's scary, and it can be daunting.

I was terrified when I left my highly successful corporate job to start something new. I could have stayed there, successful but playing small. And that's okay if that's your truth. But starting your own business is a huge, daunting task. Many of us believe the story that if we just put out a shingle, people will find us. It doesn't work that way. Being knowledgeable about cars doesn't mean you can sell them. Being a great life coach doesn't mean you can sell your services. Being an excellent hairstylist doesn't mean you can sell your skills.

The tools in this chapter are designed to help you succeed, no matter what you're selling. They're crafted to help you understand how to start talking to your customers, how to reach them, and how to get their attention. Just like the night I was rocking Halianna to sleep and it hit me like a ton of bricks, or when Jenny said, "My darling, this is not what you need to be doing," these tools are meant to create that same kind of "aha" moment for your customers.

Authentic Selling® Sales Tools Takeaways

1. **Diagnose Your Customers.** Get unstuck from the toxic marketing advice of being unable to move forward until you know your potential customers' life story.

2. **Sales Map.**

    Pain Points + Features = Benefits

    Pain Points (What's showing up in your customers' lives before they work with you)

    + Features (Your product or offer)

    = Benefits (Results after your potential customer buys from your business)

3. **"Clarity Comes from Taking Action" (Jenny Shih).** When you're stuck like molasses and confused, take action; even the wrong action provides clarity where you will get one step closer to your truth.

Chapter 5

Your Authentic Communication

Authentic Selling® Quote: "Words matter, y'all."

– Kendrick Shope

Authentic Selling® Gems from Chapter 5

- ❤ From___To_____Tool
- ❤ The Villain Tool
- ❤ The Senses Tool

Authentic Selling® Definition → Villain (in a film, novel, or play) a character whose evil actions or motives are important to the plot. "I have played more good guys than villains."

Words Matter, Y'all

I would estimate I've provided feedback on close to 10,000 sales pages over the past 13 years. It doesn't matter if you are a multi-million-dollar business owner or just getting started, almost every single sales page misses one very important part of selling. That's right, even the most seasoned salespeople struggle with getting the benefits and speaking to the transformation created by their products and services, because as we learned in the last chapter benefits are not simply the reversal of pain points but the bigger impact your product or service makes on the lives of your customers. By the end of this chapter, you will have Authentic Selling® Benefits tools that guide your sales communication. Benefits are the most challenging part of learning sales, and it takes some assistance to get your benefits to a point where they sell. Have patience with yourself. You're just getting started. You will use these Authentic Selling® Benefits tools when creating sales copy, social media, and speaking about your products and services. I go into all of this in lots of detail in the second half of this book.

Why Authentic Selling® Benefits Tools Matter

You're going to love these communication tools because they'll help you grab the attention of your prospects, highlight your products and services, and create desire for your offers. It's amazing to me how many times I can look back over the course of my life and see where just genuinely helping someone either created a massive difference in my own life or allowed me to find a new customer, or allowed me to have some wonderful thing happen that was unexpected. Just like your Authentic Selling® Sales Map, these tools can be used throughout all sales communication, including conversations meant to engage rather than convert. In fact, most conversations with prospective clients aren't about making a sale. Instead, they're about engaging the person and starting a meaningful conversation and also highlighting the true benefit of the impact of your offers.

Normal Rules of Conversation Apply

You've been communicating your whole life. You've been trying to get your point across since you were born. But you know what else applies to your Authentic Selling® Communication? Just being a good person. Simply being helpful. Now, I know you may be thinking, "Okay, Kendrick, how can actually being helpful help me make more money? How can it help me close more sales?" I mean, it sounds kind of intuitive that, well, of course, if you're a nice person, people are more likely to buy from you, but it goes a little bit deeper than that. Have you ever been to a networking event that's just gross?

Everybody's handing out their business card and telling you what they can do for you. I like to joke about that and say it's like they've channeled their inner Vanilla Ice. "If you got a problem, yo, I'll solve it." It's like, dude, I don't even know you yet. Stop selling to me. That can't feel good to anyone, both the person being sold to and the person doing the selling.

Imagine instead, the potential of your communication when it feels like helping others rather than being a bully. You can illustrate the life-changing difference of your offers with the intent of helping and being a good person. The Authentic Selling® Benefits tools help you create attention-getting conversation that converts.

The Authentic Selling® From___ To___ Tool

Often one of the best ways to show the "life-changing impact" of your product, service, coaching is to show contrast – a before and after version of what's possible. This is meant to be dramatic and to grab attention.

Creating Your Authentic Selling® From ____ Statement

Find the most painful pain point from your sales map. Think of the main thing that is driving your customers to act, seek help, make a change. Use the main desire benefit from your sales map. Think of the main thing your customer wants most as it relates to what you offer. What do they want when they put their heads on their pillows at night?

Authentic Selling® Sales Map Pain Points Take-n-Tweak from Chapter 4

- Utter lack of joy
- Constantly undermining your best intentions – setting a New Year's resolution but don't keep it?
- Vicious cycles of self-guilt
- Ridding yourself of behaviors that interrupt the life you dream about
- Finding yourself in the same ole place
- Everyone telling you how lucky you are, you have a wonderful family, and beautiful kids
- Your happiness is created outside of you
- Continuing to experience difficulties over and over

- You may be happy but the real joy is missing
- Struggling to get unstuck
- Breaking the pattern of self-sabotage
- Your happiness is dependent on external factors
- Something isn't right
- Everything feels same ole same ole
- Something is missing
- Striving for more
- Striving to succeed
- Striving for excellence
- Stumbling on happiness instead of creating it
- One-third of people who suffer from depression are not helped by the standard treatment of pharmaceuticals and/or talk therapy
- Not all depression is the same
- Overcoming feelings of helplessness and hopelessness
- Frustration of searching for customers only to end up disappointed with little money in the business bank

Creating Your Authentic Selling® To ___ Statement

Find the main desire benefit from your sales map. Think of the main thing that your customer wants more than anything as it relates to what you offer. What do they want when they put their heads on their pillows at night?

Authentic Selling® Sales Map Benefits Take-n-Tweak from Chapter 4

- Imagine the fresh possibilities
- Self-audit what's not working and begin a journey toward your "best life"
- Life is good really good

- There is laughter in your life
- There is love in your life
- There is light and family
- There are long walks that feel like a fall afternoon
- Passion
- Perseverance
- The secret to _____
- Peak performance
- Personalized approach to _____
- Work smarter
- Live better
- Intervene in your own life and get more joy, meaning, purpose, etc.
- Invaluable guidance
- Change your life
- Healing depression
- A new way forward
- Whole person approach
- Lasting relief
- Find the missing puzzle pieces for your life. It could be the difference.
- Path to lasting joy
- How to negotiate a raise or contract
- Road map to making choices that help you live the life you want
- Simple tools you can use to get what you want
- Craft a persuasive message
- How to act boldly beyond your limits so that you're happier
- Take control of your career
- Alleviate allergies
- How to actually stick to new habits

- Turn your life around
- Real-world strategies for overcoming adversity
- Effective tips to increase your happiness
- Live your healthiest life
- Empower you to eat better
- Maximize your energy
- Become a better leader
- Tips to negotiate deals and contracts
- Get ahead in the workplace and life
- Fight cancer
- Dramatically improve your life
- Never slide backward again
- Develop a healthy lifestyle – no rigid dieting required
- Make choices that serve your desires
- Never feel I have to choke down healthy food again
- Live longer
- Make an unforgettable entrance
- Live cleaner
- Live happier
- Take control, prevent symptoms of illness
- Resources for all-around healthy living
- Relieve insomnia
- Skillfully communicate
- Get out of your own way
- Detox your environment
- The ultimate plan to health
- Lessen your risk for type 2 diabetes
- Balance your hormones including the stress hormone

- How to create glowing skin and mental clarity
- Replenish your mental, physical, and emotional energy
- Relieve headaches
- Expert recipes to help with skin disorders
- Simple, natural steps to feel better and healthier
- Steps to unlock your real motivation
- Better manage your time
- Put your professional future into your own hands
- Run more effective meetings
- Simple practical ways to eat healthy delicious food for life
- How to find your purpose and pursue your life's real work
- Discover your life's purpose
- Make willpower your secret weapon without becoming exhausted
- Inspiration to become who you're meant to be
- Practical help and inspiration to help you find the job you're meant to do
- Live a life that is connected, influential, and free
- Discover why you were placed on earth
- Do more than simply exist. Live.
- Honor your calling
- More customers
- More money
- Freedom to do more of what you love daily

Creating Your Authentic Selling® From___To___Statement

It's time to put all the work you've just done together in one attention-getting statement.

Step 1 → Insert product name or service

Step 2 → from [insert your Authentic Selling® From statement you created earlier]

Step 3 → to [insert your Authentic Selling® To statement you created earlier]

"[Your product/service] will allow you to go from [pain point] to [benefit]." Consider the sharp contrast in the following examples of The Authentic Selling® From___To___ Tool.

First Example Authentic Selling® From___To___ Tool

Sales School will provide you the tools to go from the frustration of searching for customers only to end up disappointed with little money in the business bank account to more customers, making more money, and the freedom to do more of what you love every day.

Second Example Authentic Selling® From___To___ Tool

Partnering with a sleep coach will allow you to go from endless exhaustion, walking through life feeling numb, feeling like a terrible parent because no one is sleeping, to nurturing your family with the gift of sleep, feeling more energized, and even finding time to have lunch with your friend, spend time with your partner after bedtime, or have a glass of wine, and have the time to rediscover yourself.

Third Example Authentic Selling® From___To___ Tool

Life coaching will allow you to go from checking the box in your life, doing everything you should do, feeling guilty about wanting more despite how good you have it now, to stop hiding from life, relaxing more, spending more time with family/friends, and actually living every day fully.

Words matter, y'all! You can even use the Authentic Selling® From___ To___ Tool when illustrating the difference between two things using stories rather than a single sentence. The below Shope Sales Story is an example of how rather than using a couple of sentences you can also apply this same strategy to really illustrate the contrast of "from_____to____" using two stories. You may have heard "stories sell" and while that is true, the stories have to be told through a sales lens like using the "From___To___Tool. See the following example in the Shope Sales Story.

Going Speechless Meeting Heroes: A Shope Sales Story

Y'all remember in the last chapter, I shared the story of attending Rich Happy & Hot to hear Danielle LaPorte? I had a massive communication fail the first day when I had the opportunity to meet Danielle. Right now, I'm a baby in this industry. Nobody knows who I am. Oh, this little country bumpkin. I'm in New York City, the world's greatest city. I may be a Tennessee hillbilly y'all, but I am New York City in my soul. I go to the meet and greet to meet Danielle, and y'all, I love me some famous people. I do. I love meeting famous people. I'm not one who really goes speechless. I'm not one who has a hard time finding things to say. Except when I met Joe McIntyre from New Kids On the Block. My husband, he's an incredible man, was standing outside in the rain in New York City taking pictures of me all snuggled up under an umbrella with Joe McIntyre. And he said, "You were speechless. You didn't say anything. You're just all cuddled up with him after you met him in your green fur coat. And I had to speak for you." So, if you happen to be around me when I meet Joe McIntyre, I will likely go speechless.

I've met presidents and former presidents of the United States, without going speechless. But when I met Danielle LaPorte I went more than speechless, y'all. Picture it's my turn to meet Danielle, and I just want to tell her how much I loved her books, how inspired I was by her. And I get up there to meet Danielle LaPorte, and I burst into tears. I mean, I burst into tears like I can't talk, I'm crying so hard, and I didn't say a word to Danielle. I couldn't get anything out. Finally, as they're escorting me off, I turn around to Danielle LaPorte and I say, "I feel like I've met Jesus." What the ever-loving hell! I'm sobbing, tears, mascara, and snot making the perfect you look unstable accessory to carefully applied make up. I finally get words out of my mouth in between sobs and gasps, and that's what I said. I'm sure they thought I was a straight-up stalker. Not the impression you want to make. Words matter, y'all.

The Conversation That Changed Everything: A Shope Sales Story

I know I shared about getting into Marie Forleo's mastermind, and I'm in it with all of these people who were financially more successful than I was. Remember, I didn't even know what I wanted to do but I thought I was gonna be a life coach, right? And about halfway through this mastermind, a woman by the name of Jenny Shih took action, created clarity, and changed my life through helping. The most loving, generous, and gorgeous human I have ever met in my life. She's also Ivy League (she's the only person I know who is an Ivy League graduate) educated and brilliant. Jenny and I became really close and more than a decade later, I feel as close to her as I do my own family. Although we had both been through Martha Beck Life Coach Certification, Jenny and I are kind of like Paula Abdul and DJ Scat Cat from the song "Opposites Attract."

Back to the time when Jenny and I were in the mastermind we were in a Google group forum. Y'all remember Google groups? We're in this forum with all these successful entrepreneurs. Marie is in there. A couple of really famous people who worked for Comedy Central, who were giving us writing tips, and folks from Disney and all these amazing places were in there.

Jenny posted in the Google group, "Hey, I'm doing pretty well selling, but I think there's something I'm missing. It's just a hunch I have. Can anybody recommend a sales book?" And I responded with, "I can recommend a sales book, but you know, I sold for more than a decade. I was the number one sales rep for two Fortune 500 companies. I might be able to help you if you want to hop on the phone and see if I can help." So Jenny and I set up a time to hop on the phone, and I gave her what I thought were some okay pointers. We spoke for 90 minutes. And I'll have to say it says a lot about Jenny that she did not prejudge me. Because of my attention deficit disorder (ADD), I think I missed our first appointment. But she didn't prejudge me.

So we got on the phone after our second scheduled call and at the end of 90 minutes, she said, in this very Jenny, quiet way, "May I share something with you?" "Yeah, of course, anything you want." And she said, "You do not need to be a life coach. You need to be teaching this." I burst into tears in that moment and said, "I don't know what I did." Whatever I had done was so second nature to me, I didn't really know. In fact I was worried that I had not told her anything that would help her close more sales. But there's a deeper life lesson in this story about making choices that are in alignment with your values. Let's revisit two fundamental truths.

"Clarity comes from taking action." The life and business advice I learned from Jenny.

"Selling is helping." The foundational mindset that Authentic Selling® is built on.

Unlike the Joe McIntyre and Danielle LaPorte story, I did not go speechless, instead I showed up and fully took part in the conversation with Jenny. Because of that, I was able to create a business that has made millions of dollars, helped thousands of people on five continents. Fourteen years later, I still experience positive effects in my business, which extended to my personal life. Jenny became one of my best friends. Looking back, so much of my life was impacted and changed from one conversation.

My entire life was changed due to Jenny and I making choices that are aligned with our individual truths. How would you sum these two stories up using the Authentic Selling® From___To___Tool?

Authentic Selling® communication tools allow you to go from a sobbing, speechless mess, who is escorted out of important conversations, to having meaningful conversations that improve every area of your life – more money, happier, and getting more of what you want.

The Authentic Selling® Villain Tool

Villain defined (in a film, novel, or play) a character whose evil actions or motives are important to the plot. "I have played more good guys than villains."

Often one of the best ways to make something understandable to your potential customer is to make it visual. This tool is very effective for life coaches. For example, you may be known as the expert that your customers need to work on their limiting beliefs, but the customer may not even be aware they have or are experiencing issues because of limited thinking. Selling a benefit that is not visible like more happiness can be a challenge. We use this tool to make the abstract real rather than abstract. For example, thoughts can't be seen or touched, but a villain can. One way to use this tool is to make the villain the cause of the limited thinking. Now a villain doesn't have to be evil at its core, so don't get hung up on that part of the tool. This is simply a way to show your customers they are indeed struggling with, in this case, limiting beliefs and need your life coaching to help them work through that.

Life coach Martha Beck does this better than anyone I've ever seen in her bestselling book *Steering By Starlight*. In Chapter 2, Beck introduces the reader to what she calls "Wizard Vs. Lizard: The Battle for Your Brain." You guessed it. The lizard is the part of your brain broadcasting fears and limiting beliefs. While the wizard is the part of your brain that allows you to become aware that those fears are just that, fear and you can still act in spite of those fears to live a "shackled off" vs. "shackled on" life. Beck even goes as far as to have clients name their lizard and create their lizard's "top-10 playlist," which is nothing more than the limiting beliefs we tell ourselves. By making the limiting belief real, giving it form, it's easier to understand and see that we all deal with our own "inner lizard." Another example used by a client of mine is to talk about those limiting beliefs as an unweeded garden.

It's messy, tangled, the flowers of your life are unable to grow until you do the work to weed out the thoughts/weeds that are keeping your customer stuck.

The Authentic Selling® 5 Senses Tool

The 5 Senses Tool is a fun and creative way to add some personality into your copy as you communicate the benefits of your product, service, or coaching. Communicating using this tool is a powerful way to stay relevant and memorable in the minds of your potential customers.

Using the Authentic Selling® 5 Senses Tool in combination with the Authentic Selling® From_____ To_____ Tool creates impactful copy.

Example Benefit from an Authentic Selling® Sales Map

You would ask yourself the following questions using a benefit from your Authentic Selling® Sales Map.

Benefit: More Joy in Life

What does experiencing this benefit (more joy in life) look like?
Take your life from looking like Marge Simpson, chaotic and wild, to calm and beautiful like Audrey Hepburn.

What does experiencing this benefit (more joy in life) feel like?
Creating more joy allows you to stop running around, saying yes to everyone else, feeling like you never have enough time to do what you love, to wake up full of joy, gratitude, and a never-before-felt happiness in your life.

What does experiencing this benefit (more joy in life) taste like?
Your days go from being the same routine of tasting like, dull, stale cheese, to fizzing with possibility and the sweetness of champagne.

What does experiencing this benefit (more joy in life) smell like?
Being unhappy or numb is like having a wet dog in your house. It stinks and it's hard to get rid of the smell, but learning how to create more joy is like being surrounded with fresh-cut roses when you wake up every morning.

What does experiencing this benefit (more joy in life) sound like?
Unhappiness, chaos, and guilt sound like eight toddlers trying to play different instruments at one time. It's loud, obnoxiously loud. When you learn the skills to calm the chaos and experience more joy, the music of your life sounds like the most beautiful, finely tuned orchestra/music your ear has ever heard.

- Look: From chaotic like Marge Simpson to calm and beautiful like Audrey Hepburn
- Feel: From running around saying yes to everyone else to waking up full of joy and gratitude
- Taste: From stale cheese to fizzing champagne

- Smell: From wet dog to fresh-cut roses
- Sound: From eight toddlers playing different instruments to a finely tuned orchestra

Does Happiness Sell?

Too many experts are teaching that happiness isn't a benefit that can be used to convert potential clients but they are wrong. For example, I've heard more times than I can count that it's easy to sell someone on working with you when the benefit is something tangible like making more money. More money is tangible. In contrast, happiness is subjective and far less tangible. Let's clear up this belief that "happiness doesn't sell." Of course happiness sells. Who doesn't want to be happier? Helping us all live happier lives is a multi-billion-dollar industry. The experts who share that happiness isn't a benefit that is powerful enough to convert your clients simply do not know how to teach you to sell something abstract. The Authentic Selling® Benefits Tools you learned in this chapter will help you communicate the value of your offers when they are less tangible and subjective.

Authentic Selling® Tools Takeaways

- The Authentic Selling® From ___ To ___ Tool helps you show the contrast between your customer's current state and the desired outcome after using your product or service.
- The Authentic Selling® Villain Tool is particularly effective for life coaches or businesses dealing with abstract concepts. It involves giving form to the obstacles your customers face.
- The Authentic Selling® 5 Senses Tool helps you describe the benefits of your product or service using all five senses.
- As we learn these tools for authentic communication, whatever we're doing with this communication, it should never feel icky, sleazy, slimy, gross, crusty, messy, rusty, dusty. And if it does, we need to find a better way to accomplish the same outcome.

Chapter 6

Your Authentic Sales Conversations

Authentic Selling® Quote: "An Authentic Selling® conversation is nothing more than genuinely listening and telling how what you're selling can help."

– Kendrick Shope

Authentic Selling® Gems from Chapter 6

- ❖ What should never be involved in a sales conversation
- ❖ The difference between a free call and a sales call

Authentic Selling® Definition → Authentic Selling® Placebo Effect: refers to the positive impact that can come from simply sharing your problems or pain points with someone who listens and gives you their full attention. While this doesn't solve the underlying issue, it can provide short-term relief just by talking about it, as found in a 1988 study by Pennebaker, Kiecolt-Glaser, and Glaser.

It's about to get real, y'all! Actually, I think it got real already with the stories about being locked out of my house with no restroom, or my hubby's strokes, so perhaps I should say, we're going to continue with the pattern of speaking the truth – both the positive and negative. By the end of this chapter you will have what you need to have real authentic sales conversations that turn lookers into buyers! You will learn from the mistakes I see repeatedly when I watch my students sell and also receive the script that has made those same students millions of dollars.

It's time to dive into what most people actually think of when they hear the word "selling." I have been teaching this process for more than a decade.

What you are about to learn is the process that put Authentic Selling® on the map. What you're about to read in this chapter is completely opposite to what most business experts will tell you about selling and sales conversations. But I'm here to tell you that when your business begins having sales conversations using this process, you start closing more sales quickly.

Remember: the truth about selling is that when you work on improving sales skills, you should see an increase in the number of sales you make or the money in your business bank account. Why? The reason goes back to one of the very first lessons you learned at the beginning of this book.

Authentic Selling® Definition → "Selling is the exchange of money for a product or service." Translation: Without sales, your business is broke. Your business cannot make money without sales.

Too Much of a Good Thing?

Let's think of a "good thing" in your life. It could be something you love or you can't live without:

- Your car
- Favorite book
- Chapstick
- AirPods
- A dress that makes you feel pretty
- Phone

You get the idea, right? There was nothing I wanted more than a business with all the good things like making money, having customers, and creating a positive impact in the world. But making my business a success felt a bit like the song "Opposites Attract": "I take two steps forward, and you take two steps back." Like Paula Abdul and DJ Scat Cat, we try to dance with our prospects on a sales call, right?

In 2015, one of my most meaningful moments of the past 13 years occurred. I was on the *Steve Harvey Show*. My mom, husband, daughter, and my Aunt Joyce all flew up with me. It was like the Beverly Hillbillies go to NYC! I remember my husband telling me, "you deserve to be here, act like it!" Halianna was too young to be on set, so they let her watch from a special place with Blake. When I walked out onto the set, I was proud. I felt like my dreams for myself as a little girl had come true. In that moment, Halianna saw that you can start over. You can be anything you want to be and if it doesn't exist yet, create it. She did not need to look to celebrities to see proof dreams come true, but she could look to her mom who was born in a tiny town in east Tennessee, who most people discounted because of my accent, my hair, or because I just seem dumb. All things I have been told, but that story is for another time.

By the end of 2016, I had worked myself into a total state of exhaustion. I had my first panic attack because I could not get all the work done. My entire belief system about life was based on one principle: pull yourself up by your bootstraps. Well, my bootstraps were about to break, y'all, but not for another three years. I kept going for the next three years, selling.

The Authentic Selling® business model was proven. I needed to take the lead and make some hard choices about the future, but I didn't. Interestingly, here's where most people go wrong in sales conversations as well. We feel like we should be on equal footing with our prospects, so we don't take the lead on the call. And because we like to make people feel better, we give and give and give. Too many people end up coaching or giving advice for free, which makes people feel better. According to *Pennebaker and colleagues*, studies have shown that simply talking about our problems and sharing our negative emotions with someone we trust can be profoundly healing – reducing stress, strengthening our immune system, and reducing physical and emotional distress.

In other words, that creates a placebo effect where the client feels better because they've verbally vomited all over us and we've understood their problem. In that way, it's not very different from going to happy hour with your bestie. We call that the Authentic Selling® sugar pill because most placebos in pharmaceutical sales clinical trials are just a sugar pill. How effective do you think a sugar pill can be? What is surprising is they can be quite powerful . . . for a short time.

In our personal lives, that placebo effect is great. But when it comes to your business, it could be the reason you aren't converting prospects to clients. When you coach clients for free on a sales call, you are undermining your ability to sell your product or service. In my experience troubleshooting calls for clients, you're usually doing too much for free. For your sales conversations to convert, you need to do three key things.

First, there needs to be a clear separation between free and paid. When we offer a "free" discovery call or coaching call and then go into a sales pitch, that can feel like a bait and switch to clients. This problem is solved with some kickass boundaries around how long you will stay on the call (30 minutes) and what questions you will and will not answer.

Here's a great example that business coach Katie posted in our FB group: "Today I was on a call with a new client who asked me for advice on what platform she should use to promote her brand on social media. I looked her straight in the eye – or tried to, it was on Zoom – and said, 'You have to pay for me to tell you that.' I was sure she was going to get angry and end the call, but she didn't. Instead, she asked if I did paid consultations!" See what Katie did there? I call that bossing up with boundaries. I'm so proud!

The second thing that happens is that you need to take control of the call. If you're going to do free consultations, you want to make sure you can transition from talking to selling. People want to buy from experts, not amateurs. So you have to seem like you know what you're doing. Again, that sounds simple, but if you're anything like most of the students I've worked with, you are new to selling and aren't entirely comfortable with it.

The third step is where scripts come in. I know that sales scripts get a bad rap because many are sleazy, slimy, icky, and gross, but everything starts with a formula. And the same is true for Authentic Selling®.

Let's pretend that you want to make the perfect chocolate chip cookies. Apologies to all the bakers out there, I am not one. I'm one of those people who doesn't wake up knowing exactly how to make awesome chocolate chip cookies. So I use a recipe, a step-by-step process that is proven to make delicious cookies. You don't take the first step from recipe 1 and the first step from recipe 2 and the first step from recipe 3 and expect the most yummy cookies, right? The first step in all three recipes could be to add flour and then you have flour, not warm chocolate chip cookies. If you're like me you need to follow the step-by-step process, the formula, the recipe so that you have mouthwatering cookies rather than a science experiment.

Now after you make the cookies successfully a few times, you might experiment with using flaky sea salt (my fave) instead of regular salt or adding some walnuts without having a specific recipe for including them. You've followed the process enough times to know that you like a little extra sugar or less chocolate chips.

The same is true for selling and following formulas, scripts, and a step-by-step process. You can totally make this yours with your own flair but before you do, you need to understand how you create a solid sales conversation that works. Think of it as you need training wheels first, and that's what the script included in this chapter (and available online at www.copyright.com. Requests to the Publisher for permission should be addressed to the Permissions Department, John Wiley & Sons, Inc., 111 River Street, Hoboken, NJ 07030, (201) 748-6011, fax (201) 748-6008, or online at kendrickshope.com/book) will do for you.

Anyone who tells brand-new salespeople not to use a sales script is out of their mind. I mean, seriously. I have more than 18 years of sales education, tons of experience selling effectively, and have studied sales psychology . . . and I still peek at my script to prepare myself before I do a sales call with a top prospect.

What Is a Sales Conversation?

A sales conversation is known by many other names like sales consults and discovery calls. The good news is that by the end of this chapter, it doesn't matter what you call it; you're going to know how to have a sales conversation that leads people to say "yes" to what you're selling. The even better part is that closing more sales feels like helping others.

Before We Move Forward

One thing we need to get really clear before we jump into the tactical, practical steps is to define what exactly a sales conversation is, at least in the world of Authentic Selling®. I love teaching this topic so much, and I have strong feelings about what I am about to share with you. When filming training videos, I have recorded about this topic more than any other part of Authentic Selling®.

Authentic Selling® Truth: A sales conversation is not a bait and switch despite what you may have experienced or been taught.

What an Authentic Selling® Conversation Is Not

The bait: "Hey, let's have a free coffee chat where we get to know each other and how we can support one another."

The switch: "OMG, what a total coincidence that this happened at the coffee chat. I must totally tell you how I can change your life."

The bait: "Hey, want some free no-pitch advice?"

The switch: "Oh, I wasn't going to pitch you, but actually, I can help you with that issue you brought up in this free no-pitch call, but you need to pay me first."

What an Authentic Selling® Conversation Is

No bait. No switch. An Authentic Selling® conversation is real dialogue between at least two people where both parties who enter into the conversation are aware this is meant to be a talk, chat, and exchange.

Both parties enter into the conversation knowing it is a sales conversation. One person's role is the seller. I'm betting that's you. The other person's role is the prospect or potential buyer. And those people know why they're getting on the phone call.

Now, if you want to know how to have what we call mini sessions, which are free sessions that eventually lead to someone buying, that's a different class within Authentic Selling® University.

This is someone who's been to your website, heard you speak, heard you on a webinar, seen your product, test driven your product, and they're like, "Yep, I want to have a sales conversation. I am interested enough to give you my time to learn more about what you do and what your product does."

Steps to a Sales Conversation That Converts

There are 14 steps to having a sales conversation that converts to business. That may seem like a lot, but they are practical and straightforward. I'm going to tell you why each step works and give you an example of how it can be used.

Step 1: Start with a Genuine Thank You

If you remember way back in the orientation that began this book, I told you that the most of the Authentic Selling® Tools are going to start with a genuine thank you because doing so shines a light on how you're different from a sales bully. A genuine thank you allows you to make an instant connection with your potential customer.

Why it works: It puts the buyer or potential buyer's mind at ease because we, as a nation, are afraid of being sold to. Starting with a thank you acknowledges their most precious resource: time.

Example: "Thank you, [Name], for hopping on the phone [or Zoom] with me today. I appreciate people are short on time, and I value your time, and I have every intention of making the most of this time so that you get what you need today to make the best choice for your life, business, car, [whatever you're selling]."

Step 2: Make a Connection

This could also be called fast and small talk! Sounds contradictory, right? You want to show that you care about your client and have something in common with them. Remember prospects prefer to buy from people they like. By asking one "small talk" question you establish a connection but the reason we call it "fast and small talk" is this needs to last less than three minutes. We need to be respectful of the prospect's time and so we have fast small talk!

Why it works: It helps the buyer feel comfortable, mitigating the amygdala hijack and reducing fight-or-flight responses. It also shows your buyer that you remember to honor your promise to be respectful of their time. It establishes trust.

Example: "Where are you calling from? Oh, NYC? That sounds amazing! NYC is one of my favorite places to visit in the whole wide world. I love it. Broadway, the cold, city that never sleeps. Love it. Okay, I could talk about NYC all day long but I promised you to honor your time so let me set some quick expectations so there are no surprises.

Step 3: Set Expectations

This is where you put the prospect's mind at ease by telling them you're not going to pressure them because that isn't your style. Your goal is to provide your potential customer with the information they need to make the best possible choice for what they need right now. It's also the step where you begin establishing yourself as the expert, someone who doesn't need to chase a sale.

Why it works: You need to be the expert on the call. People do not want to buy from an amateur.

Example: "I'm just going to ask you some questions as we talk through today. I'm not attached to any outcome here other than getting you the answers that you need to make the best decision, whatever that is for you at this time."

Step 4: Get to the Pain

People will share their entire life story if you are available to listen. In some cases that level of detail may be needed but 9 times out of 10 it's not. Your goal is for this call to be completed in 20–30 minutes at most. You need to understand what your prospect is aware of that they are experiencing that causes them to have this conversation with you today.

Why it works: Understanding what motivates the customer to seek a solution is crucial.

Example: "What prompted you to reach out today?"

Step 5: Thanks for Sharing

We often forget that our prospect likely just shared something personal with you and you are likely a stranger. Before we jump straight into selling them we need to show them they are more than a number to us.

Why it works: It acknowledges the trust the customer has shown by sharing their pain.

Example: "Thanks for sharing that with me."

Step 6: Tactical Empathy + Mirroring

Step 6 has two parts and both are needed to do step 6 correctly.

First. remember in the first chapters we discussed that everyone has a bad sales experience to share? We've come to expect sales conversations where, as the potential buyer, we have to be on guard, watching to make sure we do not get swindled. Tactical Empathy is a tool used by the hostage negotiation teams at the Federal Bureau of Investigation (FBI) to calm down someone who has taken hostages. It defuses the anxiety and shows that you are listening and you're not interested in telling someone they are wrong but instead that you are fully present for this conversation.

Why it works: Mirroring their words back shows understanding.

Example: "I understand how it feels to have just had a baby and want to walk into your class reunion feeling hotter at 40 than you did at 18."

Step 7: Start Selling

This step is where you take the reigns of the call and show that you not only understand but that you also are an expert in the area your prospect is struggling with. It shows the potential client you know exactly how to help them or what to provide.

Why it works: It transitions the conversation to your solution.

Example: "That's exactly why I created [Product Name]."

Step 8: Pattern Interrupt with Features

Why it works: Keeps the buyer's attention by breaking the pattern.

Example: "What's included in [Product Name] is: Number one, [Feature]. Number two, [Feature]. Number three, [Feature]."

Step 9: From Pain to Benefit

Why it works: Connects features to outcomes.

Example: "All of that means you have what you need to go from [Pain Point] to [Benefit]."

Step 10: Pattern Interrupt with Benefits

Why it works: Reinforces the benefits of your product or service.

Example: "The biggest changes you can expect to see are: Number one, [Benefit]. Number two, [Benefit]. Number three, [Benefit]."

Step 11: Ask Questions

Why it works: Ensures the buyer is on the same page and clears up any confusion before discussing investment.

Example: "What questions do you have?"

Step 12: Share the Investment

Why it works: Positions the cost as an investment in the buyer's future.

Example: "The investment is [Amount]. We can break that up into [Number] payments of [Amount]."

Step 13: Address Objections

Why it works: Prepares you for common objections and how to handle them.

We will cover this in the next chapter.

Step 14: The Close

Why it works: Wraps up the conversation positively and leaves the door open for further questions.

Example: "Thank you so much for hopping on the phone with me today. As you come up with other questions, let me know what they are, and I'll be in touch."

Authentic Selling® Conversations Takeaways

1. **Listen.** Any sales expert who is good at what they do will talk about the importance of really listening to your potential customers. Listening enhances potential customer satisfaction because a prospect who feels listened to is more likely to be satisfied with the interaction, whether or not they make a purchase. This positive experience can lead to future business, referrals, and a positive reputation for your brand.

2. **Understand, no really understand.** Approach each call with the mindset of understanding and solving your customer's needs rather than just making a sale. We do this with Tactical Empathy + Mirroring.

   Numerous positive things happen when you use Tactical Empathy but one of the most powerful is that you avoid misunderstandings that can lead to lost sales and confusion. By using the words "I understand how it feels" followed by mirroring your prospect's words you demonstrate empathy, signaling to the customer that you are interested in their specific situation and not just making a sale. This can differentiate you from competitors who may focus solely on pushing their products.

3. **Understand the Goal of a Sales Call.** Sales calls are more than just transactions; they are opportunities to build trust and establish long-term relationships. As you continue to develop your skills, you'll find that your calls become more natural, effective, and rewarding. You will use the script less and have the confidence to adjust it so it feels the most natural, no different than having a conversation with a friend.

4. **Mirror Mirror.** When I was in corporate sales school one of the most embarrassing things I've ever done, and y'all know by this point I've done a lot of embarrassing things, but our instructors

would challenge us to deliver our sales presentation in front of the mirror nightly. UGGGGGH! I know that sounds cheesy and a little painful to watch yourself deliver a sales presentation. The point was the instructors knew how important it was to practice and become comfortable. The following day our instructors would have us role play with another person in front of everyone. Practicing in front of the mirror was an attempt to get us comfortable with saying the words in the script.

If you've ever been on a stage speaking, singing, dancing, or acting you know that the goal is to perform so much in rehearsal that everything is muscle memory to the point where you don't even have to think about what comes next. You know the next line, verse, step, stanza, it's just natural as a result of all the rehearsals. You need this to feel second nature to you so that you're not even thinking about the script as you have the conversation.

Authentic Selling® Challenge

I'm going to challenge you here to do something that isn't fun but it will help you close more sales and make more money. Find someone to practice the sales call with; trust the redhead, you will see success much faster by getting comfortable with the script so it becomes second nature, similar to performers. Will you accept the challenge to practice the script either in front of a mirror or with other people and practice it until you're comfortable?

Three Key Actions for Successful Sales Conversations

1. **Separate Free from Paid:** Establish clear boundaries for free and paid services to avoid bait-and-switch scenarios.
2. **Control the Call:** Transition from talking to selling by using scripts to appear knowledgeable and professional.
3. **Use Scripts:** Emphasize the importance of scripts for new salespeople to ensure successful sales conversations.

Steps to a Sales Conversation That Converts

1. Start with a Genuine Thank You: Acknowledge the prospect's time.
2. Make a Connection: Help the prospect feel comfortable.
3. Set Expectations: Be the expert on the call.
4. Get to the Pain: Understand the customer's motivations.
5. Thanks for Sharing: Acknowledge their trust.
6. Tactical Empathy + Mirroring: Use the words I understand how it feels followed by mirroring their words to show understanding.
7. Start Selling: Transition to your solution.
8. Pattern Interrupt with Features: Keep attention by listing features.
9. From Pain to Benefit: Connect features to outcomes.
10. Pattern Interrupt with Benefits: Reinforce product benefits.
11. Ask Questions: Ensure clarity before discussing investment.
12. Share the Investment: Present the cost as an investment.
13. Address Objections: Prepare for and handle common objections.
14. The Close: Wrap up positively, leaving the door open for further questions.

Chapter 7

Your Authentic Close

Authentic Selling® Quote: "An objection is redirection, nothing more."
– Kendrick Shope

Authentic Selling® Gems from Chapter 7

❖ You will learn how to work through any objections that impede the close.

❖ What to do when you hear the most dreaded words in selling.

❖ Amateur sales tools to avoid.

Authentic Selling® Vocabulary Words

Doubt:

1. uncertainty of belief or opinion that often interferes with decision-making

Objection:

1. potential customers saying no or not right now to a product/service

2. potential customers expression of a lack of trust or hesitation in a product/service

Values:

1. the beliefs people have, especially about what is right and wrong and what is most important in life, that control their behavior

Authentic Selling® Key Takeaway:

By the end of this chapter, you're going to go from wondering how to handle the most dreaded words in sales, to having a full understanding and proven words to authentically close more sales with integrity.

The Most Dreaded Words in Sales

What the heck do you do now? That's where we are in your Authentic Selling® process or as I often refer to it "the most dreaded words in sales."

"I can't afford it!"

By the end of this chapter, you're going to go from wondering how to handle the most dreaded words in sales, to having a full understanding and proven words to authentically close more sales.

Nothing stops a potential deal, close, or sale faster than bringing up money. I understand no one wants to push people into investing in a product/service that they can't afford. You also need to be in control of the sales conversation the entire time. Your customers want to buy from someone who believes in what they are selling.

Why It Matters

Too many people with incredible offers that make a powerful difference in the lives of others give up when faced with an objection from a prospect. This chapter teaches you the exact words to say to move from objection to redirecting the conversation back to the life-changing difference made by your offer.

The Anatomy of an Authentic Selling® Sales Conversation

Think of an Authentic Selling® sales conversation as nothing more or less than an exchange of information.

- Prospect/potential customer is experiencing an area of dissatisfaction in life, health, work.

- You as the salesperson share what you know of those areas of dissatisfaction.
- Your prospect/potential customer knows they are seen, heard, and understood because you shared the information.
- You as the salesperson then share the details (features) of your product/service.
- You as the salesperson then share what will be different for the prospect/potential customer due to your product or service.
- Your prospect/potential customer shares questions, hesitations, or objections.
- You as the salesperson provide another way of looking at the hesitation or objection so that we've provided all that is needed to make the best choice for them at this time.
- You as the salesperson check in on the prospect/potential customer making them again feel seen, heard, and understood.

Your Heart Doc Called and You Can't Afford It: A Shope Sales Story

I once called on cardiologists, who are notoriously challenging to engage. As I share this Shope Sales Story, it's important to note the type of selling I used here is a bit on the more aggressive side of my personal Authentic Selling® Sales Guardrail (I talked about Sales Guardrails in a previous chapter). While it may feel more direct than you are currently comfortable selling, I had earned the right to have the tough conversation, ask hard questions of this cardiologist, and I was entirely comfortable and within my comfort zone for my guardrail.

I was selling a heart drug, let's call it Drug A, which belonged to a class of medications that were the first line of treatment after a heart attack. Drug A had "mortality data," meaning that in a head-to-head study against Drug B, it was statistically proven to help patients live longer.

So, I walked into the office of a cardiologist who had been practicing longer than I'd been alive, probably double my lifetime. I said, "Dr. X, how are you today?"

He replied, "Well, I'm doing well, Kendrick. How are you?"

"Great, thank you. Now, Dr. X, let me ask you a question. If your wife, God forbid, had a heart attack, which drug would you put her on post-heart attack, Drug A or Drug B?"

Without hesitation, he said, "I'd put her on Drug A."

"Okay, great. Why is that?"

He explained, "Because of the mortality data, and this, and that."

Pause right there.

We Interrupt This Shope Sales Story for This Record Scratch Moment

When my customer Dr. X shared his patients were not able to afford Drug A, my product, this is what I call a record scratch moment. Imagine you're watching the best episode of *Buffy The Vampire Slayer* and at the same time a major event worldwide happens. The next thing you hear is, "We interrupt this program with breaking news." A record scratch moment feels a bit like a needle scratching across a record player that gets most people's attention.

Back to Your Regularly Scheduled Shope Sales Story

Surprised, I asked, "What do you mean they can't afford it? Are they telling you that directly, or calling you after the fact? Because I'll give them samples if you think it's the best drug for them. We'll find a way. I'll call the company, do whatever it takes."

But Dr. X clarified, "No, Kendrick. As you know, we practice in an indigent area, and we don't have time to field all the callbacks from patients who can't afford the medication."

He was trying to protect his staff from being inundated with calls they couldn't handle, even though he believed Drug A was the right choice for most of his heart attack patients, who comprised about 80% of his practice.

I replied, "Okay, thank you for sharing that with me. I understand you feel your patients in this indigent area can't afford Drug A. I also understand it feels as if your staff will be inundated with callbacks they do not have the time to handle." Notice, I didn't pounce. I had empathy.

"Dr. X, where Drug A is indicated and if affordability wasn't an issue is this the drug you would prescribe for your patients who have suffered a heart attack?"

"Yes, absolutely," he confirmed.

"Great. Here's what I'm going to do. I'll go talk to M, your nurse who handles the callbacks. She and I will figure out a system to ensure the patients you want on Drug A can get on it and stay on it, without you having to deal with the administrative burden. Obviously, you'll still have to write the prescriptions, but nurse M and I will make it happen behind the scenes."

And we did. Dr. X became one of our biggest prescribers of Drug A, which was also a win for his patients because Drug A was proven to extend lives compared to other drugs in a similar class. Taking the time to understand your customer's unique challenges allows you to find a workable solution.

With that one question, I knew Dr. X understood the data. I didn't need to educate him on why Drug A was better; he had just told me. So, I decided it was time to get direct with Dr. X. I said, "Dr. X, that's fantastic. So, why aren't your patients who have experienced a heart attack leaving the hospital on Drug A? The samples aren't moving off your shelf, and I know it's not being written despite what you just shared about mortality data."

He admitted, "Well, Kendrick, my patients can't afford it."

An Amateur's Sales Tool

In contrast, too many sales experts teach that using guilt is a fast way to agree with your potential customer by using shame as a tool. It is true that shame/guilt does work as a tool for overcoming/working through objections, and to close more sales. But shame and guilt are an amateur's sales tool. It never leads to anyone of integrity leaving a sales conversation feeling empowered, excited, and ready to get to work. Instead it leaves most people feeling buyer's remorse, icky, sleazy, slimy, gross. I'm willing to bet if you're reading this book, that is not how you want your customers who have just purchased from you feeling! What does shame/guilt look like when it's being used to help you close?

"If you give up your Starbucks, you can apply that money toward this new product that is going to change your life."

"If it was really important to you, there is always a way to work it out."

"Experts teach you that you have to make people feel uncomfortable."

"Your daughter deserves to have a mom who is healthy."

Your Customer's Money Is None of Your Business

Do you want your doctor treating you based on appearances? "Oh, she's wearing hole-y jeans. She can't afford this drug or treatment." Of course not. Do you want salespeople making snap judgments like, "They're just a [insert stereotype]. They can't afford this truck, purse, or whatever, so I won't even show it to them." It's arrogant and you are doing a disservice to your customers when you think you know someone's financial situation better than they do.

You may be thinking, "Yeah, okay, I got it." But one of people's biggest issues in sales is meddling with other people's money, saying they can't afford something, believing that their money is your business. It's not. As the seller, your job is to talk about the life-changing benefits of your product or service. It's the customer's job to figure out how to pay for what you're selling.

As sure as my hair is red, 9 out of 10 customers can figure out a way to make it happen if they want it bad enough. Your job is to show them the life-changing benefit of your product or service without using tools of manipulation. Your customers are adults, show them the respect they deserve by providing them with the opportunity to make the best choice at this time regarding if now is the time to invest. While money will be the most common objection you hear, it's not the only one you will hear.

Common Objections

- "I need to think about it."
- "I can't afford it."
- "My spouse said no."
- "I need to finish all those classes that I've already purchased before I spend more money."
- "I'm not in the market for a new car right now."

According to Sales Legend Zig Ziglar, There Are Five Things That Stop a Sale:

- No need
- No desire
- No money
- No trust
- No hurry

It is important to note that in times of scarcity, like the COVID-19 pandemic, this sales key takeaway may not always be accurate. People are suffering and scared making them less likely to invest. It is even more important to note that in these times of scarcity, businesses that use fear-based selling, guilt, or traditional sales bullying will not thrive. Instead those businesses that sell with authenticity and empathy will prosper, helping those who need your work when it matters most. If you begin questioning if you should be selling or if it's ethical because of external forces, remember that your customers NEED your work. Selling is the bridge that connects those in need to the solution – your offer. Authentic Selling® allows you to use empathy rather than bullying someone into buying. When you lead with empathy rather than pushing, you create customers for life and you change your customers' lives.

Dangerously Directionless: A Shope Sales Story

Authentic Selling® Confession: Out of all the embarrassing stories I've shared with you, I'm the most embarrassed of what you're about to read.

Selling isn't the only place we can encounter objections, right? It takes confidence to hear the hesitations of others and remain sure of your next step. A lack of confidence will suck the air out of your dreams, business, products/services, and just about anything. Isn't it ironic that your most confident and successful times are often followed by doubt, lack of clarity, and uncertainty. Authentic Selling® was growing faster than I could keep up with. My personal goal, as the CEO, was to have a $10 million year. I had a highly skilled team in place, and things were rocking and rolling in a wonderful way. Our clients/customers were experiencing the best years financially they've ever had, and word of mouth was spreading about the "fiery southern redhead who was an expert at sales." Then it happened.

The place was Denver, Colorado, and the senior team of Authentic Selling® was there to map out the Authentic Selling® business plan for the following year. The location is important only because it adds some humor to the near destruction of my dream. Something about the "Mile High City" and I do not mix. I could not breathe well, and I drank gallons and gallons of water, at least four times as much water compared to a normal day closer to sea level. As the senior team sat down and began what they called an "intervention," I had had so much water that I was running back and forth to the restroom. These people who were trying to have what seemed like a loving conversation out of concern for me had to pause every seven minutes for me to say, "Sorry y'all, I will be right back." The only thing worse would have been if I were on a stage and that happened.

Here we were in the thirstiest city in the world, celebrating the successes of the past year and planning how Authentic Selling® would get to $10 million in sales. Instead, my team had set up an intervention. They shared with me that they would not continue to watch me work as hard as I had been because they were worried about my health. Sitting in Denver, I had a record scratch moment that left me still thirsty, but I allowed it to plant a seed of doubt that grew into poison. Without going into specifics, Authentic Selling® came out of that meeting 100% different than it had been before. Looking back on this time, I understand the reason for this intervention. In fairness, I inherited a driven work ethic from my father, one that pushes beyond reason. I have struggled with respecting my own boundaries, giving too much only to end up beyond exhausted, crashing on the couch for 24 hours straight. Even more important, the people in that room shared that $10 million was not doable with the existing business structure. They were correct.

What got Authentic Selling® to this rapidly growing success would not get it to the next round of goals. What I know now as you read this is a result of that intervention. I know I failed everyone in that room, Authentic Selling®, my customers, and myself. I know we did not analyze what changing the structure to "scale" would require financially. I know we did not consider how I would feel and show up without as much engagement between myself and the customers. In hindsight, I removed the magic, the spark, the part that makes Authentic Selling® stand out and differentiate itself.

Authentic Selling® Confession: I found myself at a crossroads where I fully considered lighting a match to the past decade of work, giving up, quitting, and walking away from the #1 sales process in the world. I went from confident to full of doubts, questions instead of answers, and worrying if I was good enough. It was the darkest time in my business, and that doubt grew. I second-guessed nearly all the choices I made, and I was no leader to my team. Within three years, while visiting my favorite place in the world, New York City, I found myself overwhelmed by the most excruciating pain of my life, screaming in agony, fully ready to give in and give up.

Failure to know how to handle objections in life and business creates apprehension. Specifically, letting the sales objections run the show can make even the most confident person feel awkward. Just like I needed someone to yank me out of my own way in that intervention, all salespeople need a step-by-step process for handling objections like a boss because when you are able to take care of people's hesitations, they are more likely to trust you.

Authentic Selling® Truth: Taking care of prospects' hesitations with integrity rather than being a bully will increase trust. In Chapter 1, you learned that increased trust will lead to increased purchasing from your potential customers.

Authentic Selling® Drive With Five

Each chapter in this book, every lesson, and all the tools are starting to come together and build into one proven sales process. Your Authentic Selling® Sales Process changes selling to an activity that feels like helping, allowing you to find and close more customers, and create more freedom in your day-to-day. When you encounter an objection, you will rely on the proven Authentic Selling® Drive With Five. Your main five steps will be the same for each of the closes/tools for working through objections you learn later in this chapter.

Let's look back at what happens immediately before you use Drive With Five in your sales conversations. You're in the middle of an Authentic Sales Conversation using what you learned in Chapter 6.

Setting the Scene

Your potential customer shares with you after you share the investment of your product/service, "I can't afford your coaching program right now."

Recognizing this as an objection and knowing that your customers' money is none of your business, you realize this is an opportunity to stand out and redirect the conversation.

Authentic Selling® Drive With Five

Step 1: Start with a Genuine Thank You

Step 2: Tactical Empathy

Step 3: Mirroring

Step 4: Emotional Support Using Your Value Proposition

Step 5: Choose one of the tools for working through objections/tools for closing

Authentic Selling® Drive With Five Explained
Step 1: Start with a Genuine Thank You

"Thank you for sharing that with me."

Why Step 1 Works

Most salespeople do not stop to consider what a big deal of trust it is for someone, who is most likely somewhat of a stranger, to share with you their financial situation. Taking a second to thank them for trusting you with that information diffuses the uncomfortable feeling and awkwardness that can come from this moment in the sales process.

Step 2: Tactical Empathy

"I understand how it feels to . . ."

Why Step 2 Works

Tactical Empathy is used by FBI hostage negotiation teams and was coined by famous FBI, Scotland Yard, and Harvard-trained negotiations expert Chris Voss. Here I use it to emphasize the importance of using Tactical Empathy in sales. Tactical Empathy has been studied in various forms for years, even dating back to the foundations of psychotherapy and psychology. In essence, it just requires a little common sense. In the South, we call this "you get more flies with honey than with vinegar." While the saying might be odd, the point is clear: people are more likely to trust you, buy from you, and give you their money if they like you and feel seen and understood. This is not about bulldozing or projecting your feelings onto someone else; it's about taking the time to understand where the other person is coming from.

An important distinction here is to note that when you use Tactical Empathy, you actually use the words "I understand how it feels" after an objection is shared. Think about it. Your prospect/potential customer has shared a potential financial hesitation/objection. I don't know about you, but sharing that I feel my finances are tight and sharing that with a stranger isn't something I enjoy doing. The last thing I want to experience at that moment is someone making me feel bad about myself after I share something so personal. Note the use of the word feel here. Instead of saying "I understand you can't afford this program right now," we acknowledge how the potential customer or prospect _feels_: "I understand that you feel . . . you can't afford this coaching program right now." The word "feel" makes all the difference.

Step 3: Mirroring

"Thank you for sharing that with me. I understand how it feels to (insert your clients mirroring words)."

Incorrect Mirroring

Imagine you've created an offer that helps women under 60 lose weight. On a sales call, you ask the potential customer/prospect, "What prompted you to schedule this call?" Your prospect replies, "I want to go to my high school reunion in three months looking hotter at age 50 than I did at age 18. I have a little baby weight to lose, and I am ready to get it off, strut into that reunion, and turn some heads." Now you're a good student, and you think to yourself, "I'm going to use that Mirroring thing that Kendrick said was so hard to use."

You start your Drive With Five by saying, "Thank you for sharing that. I understand what it's like to feel you want to lose some weight before you attend your high school reunion."

Is this a good use of Mirroring? No, instead, you need to repeat back the exact words that the potential customer used in answer to your question, ensuring that you eliminate potential communication errors.

Let's have a redo, shall we?

Correct Mirroring

On a sales call, you ask the potential customer/prospect, "What prompted you to schedule this call?" Your prospect replies, "I want to go to my high school reunion in three months looking hotter at age 50 than I did at age 18. I have a little baby weight to lose, and I am ready to get it off, strut into that reunion, and turn some heads."

Now you're a good student, and you think to yourself, "I'm going to use that Mirroring thing that Kendrick said was so hard to use." You start your Drive With Five by saying, "Thank you for sharing that. I understand what it's like to want to go to my high school reunion in three months looking hotter at age 50 than I did at age 18. I have a little baby weight to lose, and I am ready to get it off, strut into that reunion, and turn some heads."

Mirroring is commonly taught in many sales programs, including the corporate sales schools where I graduated. It often gets overlooked because it seems so simple. As a result, many people do it incorrectly. So, let's ensure we understand how to effectively use Mirroring, at least from a language perspective, right now.

Why Step 3 Works

Mirroring is a technique where you copy the words used to share an objection by a potential customer. This method helps build rapport and create a sense of familiarity and trust, as people tend to feel more comfortable with those who seem similar to them. The goal of Mirroring is to make the customer feel understood and at ease, which can facilitate better communication and increase the likelihood of a successful sale.

Step 4: Emotional Support Using Your Value Proposition

"You're not alone, it's not a fun place to be when you see a program that can change your life, health, business, confidence, weight, etc., and feel you can't afford it."

A value proposition is all about what your product or service does for customers, it's a benefit from your sales map. "Show your customer they are not alone" is saying your business offers emotional support and connection, making customers feel understood. It speaks to those who appreciate empathy and personal touch, highlighting a key benefit you provide.

Why Step 4 Works

The old way of selling teaches to use guilt, shame, and to assume you know what's better in life and financially for your customers. We were told it was our job as salespeople to help the customer see clearly the impact saying they can't afford your offer is creating in their lives. Selling using guilt and shame is an amateur's sales technique and is one of the reasons many have icky, sleazy, slimy, gross, crusty, musty, and dusty feelings about selling. Assuming that you know your customers' needs or finances better than they do is arrogant at best. We're at a time in history where humans are more sensitive and are quicker to anger. Showing off the value of your product or service while offering empathy and emotional support is a much better way to redirect your conversation after an objection is shared.

Step 5: Insert One of the Below Tools

- Tool 1: Let Them Off the Hook
- Tool 2: Do Nothing and Sell in Follow-Up
- Tool 3: Expert Recommendations
- Tool 4: Make It Personal
- Tool 5: Call Their Bluff
- Tool 6: Head On
- Tool 7: Discount the Objection
- Tool 8: Back to Desire
- Tool 9: Imagine
- Tool 10: When Is a Good Time? (Great Tool for Corporate Selling or Telemarketing)
- Tool 11: How to Get a Phone Number (Corporate Sales Tool)

Tools for Overcoming Objections

Remember, you're going to use your Drive With Five steps 1–4 before you insert one of the these tools for overcoming objections:

Tool 1: Let Them Off the Hook

"Thank you for sharing. I understand you feel now isn't a good time to invest in [insert what you're selling]. I respect that you have a better grasp of your finances than anyone, and I'm not about to be a high-pressure salesperson and push [insert whatever you're selling] on you. I've been in business long enough to know what phenomenal results my clients get, but I also realize that one of the fastest ways to lose your trust is to push you. I respect your decision and thank you for your time. Are there any other questions I can answer today about this?"

Tool 2: Do Nothing and Sell in Follow-Up
"Thank you for sharing. I understand you feel now isn't a good time to invest in a new car. I respect that you know what's best for you and your [insert what you do]. Are there any other questions I can answer today about your Mercedes?"

Tool 3: Expert Recommendations
"Thank you for sharing. I understand you feel now isn't a good time to [Mirroring their words]. I've been doing this work for a long time, and I see many people who succeed and some who don't. I love to give tangible tips for everyone, so as your coach, I would tell you the best way to make progress toward [insert what they want here (making money, increasing productivity, creating a life you love, etc.)] is to [insert what you're selling here (a class, an event, a private coaching experience, work privately)]. Even if it's not me, I encourage you, when you're ready to invest in working with someone, this is the way to get you toward your desired results. Are there any other questions I can answer today about [insert what you do (your sales process, branding, your health, etc.)]"?

Tool 4: Make It Personal
"Thank you for sharing. I understand you feel [Mirroring their words]. What is missing from this product or service? What would you like to see included that isn't currently included?"

Tool 5: Call Their Bluff
"Thank you for sharing. I understand what it feels like to [Mirroring their words]. May I ask you a couple of questions? Am I the type of person you want to do business with or learn from? Does the product or service get you where you want to go? Great, thank you for talking it out with me. So I am the type of person you want to do business with, and the product or service gets you where you want to go. What's missing from this experience? I want this for you. How do we create a partnership that works so you can [insert benefit]? I'm not trying to sell you here, but money aside, does it get you where you want to go? . . . If no . . . What would you like to see included

in this service that is not currently here? Are there any other questions I can answer today about [insert what you do (your sales process, branding, your health, etc.)]?"

Tool 6: Head On

"Thank you for sharing. I understand you feel [Mirroring their words]. Over the course of doing this work for a while, I know people pay for what they value. I'm a straight shooter, so shoot me straight. Tell me what's missing from this product or service. Where do you feel uncertain about it?"

Tool 7: Discount the Objection

"Thank you for sharing. I understand you feel [Mirroring their words]. Your story reminds me of my own story. I remember when I paid $25,000 to work with a mastermind when I was just starting a business. It was such a large investment, and we didn't have that kind of money at that time. It didn't make sense. I had just quit a secure job with tons of benefits. I was blowing through my savings all in the name of following my dream, but I knew in my gut that I was meant to make this investment. It was hard. It was not at all what I expected, but it was exactly what I needed. I would not be here today without that investment because of what I learned and the connections I made. What I have found is that sometimes saying yes to something that makes no sense on paper is one of the best ways to create results because your rear is on the line, and you have no choice but to succeed, so I totally understand what you are saying because I've been there. I also see my clients do this all the time when they feel like they can't afford it, but somehow they find a way, and something happens when those clients find a way. It's like a fire is lit inside of their soul and passions. Those clients go at a new level of intensity that allows them to succeed faster than they realized was possible. I respect what you're saying but felt led to share that story with you because I know what would have happened if I had said no to my opportunity all those years ago. I'm here to help you make the best decision for you at this time. Are there any other questions I can answer today about [insert what you do (your sales process, branding, your health, etc.)]?"

Tool 8: Back to Desire

"Let me ask you a question: as a result of investing in [insert product name], what do you need to accomplish?" [Assuming your offer delivers what they are looking for, then proceed with the following:] "Thank you for sharing with me that you're looking to accomplish [insert what potential customer said (use exact words)]. I can assure you that is the exact reason I created [insert product name]/became a life coach/[(insert what you do)]. You will absolutely receive what you need to accomplish. What other questions do you have?"

Tool 9: Imagine

"Thank you for sharing. I understand you feel [Mirroring their words]. Let's do a little exercise. Put the money aside for just a second and imagine what it is going to feel like [insert benefit (be super descriptive)]. That's exactly what you're going to be able to do with the tools that you learn inside of [insert product or offer name]. It's about more than money. It's about more than running a business (or whatever fits as it relates to your business). Any way we can make this happen today?"

Tool 10: When Is a Good Time? (Great Tool for Corporate Selling or Telemarketing)

"Thank you for sharing. I understand that you feel you're too busy and now isn't a good time. When would be a good time to follow up?"

Tool 11: How to Get a Phone Number (Corporate Sales Tool)

Instead of asking, "Can I have a phone number?" say, "Thank you for sharing. I understand you feel [Mirroring their words]. What's the best number to reach you at, and I will follow up when you have a bit more time."

Authentic Selling® Tools Takeaways

1. **Authentic Selling® Drive With Five Process For Working Through Potential Client Objections**
   - Step 1: Start with a Genuine Thank You

- Step 2: Tactical Empathy
- Step 3: Mirroring
- Step 4: Emotional Support Using Your Value Proposition
- Step 5: Chose one of the tools for working through objections/tools for closing
  - Tool 1: Let Them Off the Hook
  - Tool 2: Do Nothing and Sell in Follow-Up
  - Tool 3: Expert Recommendations
  - Tool 4: Make It Personal
  - Tool 5: Call Their Bluff
  - Tool 6: Head On
  - Tool 7: Discount the Objection
  - Tool 8: Back to Desire
  - Tool 9: Imagine
  - Tool 10: When Is a Good Time? (Great Tool for Corporate Selling or Telemarketing)
  - Tool 11: How to Get a Phone Number (Corporate Sales Tool)

2. **Nine times out of ten, your customer will say it's about price:** "I can't afford it" – the most dreaded words in sales. It's your job, as the seller, to try to uncover what it's really about. Most times, people are happy to pay whatever price if they are convinced you can deliver what they're looking for.

Chapter 8

Your Authentically Written Sales Page Copy

Authentic Selling® Quote: "Your competition is for your customer's attention not with other business."

– Kendrick Shope

Authentic Selling® Gems from Chapter 8

- ❖ Learn what to do if you're stuck in writer's block, staring at a blank page.
- ❖ Uncover the secrets to getting Authentic Testimonials that sell.
- ❖ Understand silent closes and how to use them to increase your sales.

You learned in Chapter 6 how to have sales conversations that convert, work through objections without being a bully, and close sales authentically. But what about writing sales copy?

What exactly is written copy? It is a page on a website with the intention of stopping the dreaded doom scroll. It's to get the attention of your potential customers and create sales for your business. Follow-up communication, blogs, and even social media are examples of written copy.

Authentic Selling Pro Tip → This is a dense chapter, and I say that to give you fair warning. We want to ensure you take this step-by-step, like my friends at New Kids On the Block. Specifically, we're going to take this in 10 steps.

No more staring at a blank page. No more wondering where to start.

Actually, we're going to pull our Sales Map out from Chapter 4. It doesn't matter what kind of copy you're starting with. Taking the time to first create an Authentic Selling® Sales Map will make the writing process go so much easier and move at a much quicker speed.

Authentic Selling® Refresher → Your Sales Map is your customers' pain points + features of your product or service = benefits of your product or service.

Before we jump into the 10 steps, let's set a couple of ground rules that will keep you focused while writing sales copy.

To write the best copy, you have to be aware of your customer's time, keeping things simple, and your customer's attention, interest, and desire. What does that mean? Glad you asked!

Your Customer's Time

Your customers are like my customers. No matter what you're selling, they are busy and likely being pulled in opposing directions all day. They have cell phones going off, iWatches sending alerts, Samsungs beeping, kids asking what's for dinner, spouses saying they'll be home late, Netflix shows to watch, work to do, bosses calling. I mean, it's exhausting just to think about, right? So I can assure you that your customers, when reading your sales page, are likely multitasking.

Research shows that less than 2% of the entire world's population can actually multitask. That means 98% of people impair their ability to think and comprehend when multitasking. According to Real Simple magazine, when people are multitasking, they have the same brain capacity as somebody who is high from smoking marijuana.

As we write copy, we have to think about how we grab attention. How we create desire. Because our customer's brain capacity is impaired! You have to be in that attention-grabbing frame of mind as you create copy.

K.I.S.S Tool → *Keep It Super Simple*

We've got to cover a sales principle that many experts teach, called the Kiss Principle.

I learned the K.I.S.S. Tool like this: Keep It Simple Stupid. I hated that. It's just mean. Who wants to be "stupid"? It pushed my Authentic Selling® Sales Guardrail in a really negative way so I found a better way to achieve the same results only without the ick.

K.I.S.S. = Keep It Super Simple. It's time to get romantic with your sales copy, which sounds ridiculous but you're more likely to remember this sales tool now! Your copy has to be so simple that someone who is multitasking understands your message, understands what you can do for them, and it grabs their attention enough for you to hook them in to keep reading. Too many people get hung up on creating perfect copy. That is a mistake and you will miss opportunities to get out there and connect with your customers. Your copy doesn't need to win a Pulitzer Prize. It doesn't need to be super complicated. In fact, if it is, you are pushing your buyers away. I don't care if you sell to PhD-level people. If they're reading it when they're multitasking, and they are, it's got to be K.I.S.S. Keep It Super Simple. Because when we're multitasking our brains are distracted; we don't give our full attention to a single thing, like reading sales copy, a new idea, or a plan.

A Shope Sales Story

Keep It Super Simple applies not only to selling and writing copy but also to taking care of your business, and achieving business growth.

Authentic Selling® Truth → When used in the Authentic Selling® world, simple doesn't mean easy. Instead simple means uncomplicated. It's fair to say I got away from the Keep It Super Simple approach to business and sales after that meeting in Denver. While I was still successful, I saw my numbers start to decline while my work hours skyrocketed. You may be thinking here comes the same ole story from burnout to refreshed and reinvigorated. That's not exactly what happened. Things are about to change and get complicated y'all.

A few years ago all of the planets in our world lined up to form the best quarter of my life. January – the first half of March, I was in NYC more than I was at home in Knoxville. But let me go back a few months before that; I'm speaking one day and my cell phone was on silent. But like a good momma, I can tell if Halianna is calling even when it's on silent. We have a family rule not to call mom when I'm speaking.

That day in October, Halianna called at least seven times while I was delivering that keynote. It goes without saying, I was scared, really scared something was wrong. As soon as I was off stage, I called Halianna back and she screams, "Have you heard?" Turns out Aaron Tveit was returning to *Moulin Rouge The Musical* January 17. I've shared that we are massive supporters of Broadway, but Aaron happened to be Halianna's fave and he was coming back. Halianna called all those times and told me she wanted to go to NYC as much as possible during Aaron's return January–May and we did just that.

January 17 came and you better believe we were present to see Aaron's return in *Moulin Rouge The Musical*. Halianna and I had a trip to remember, it was incredible. When I got back to Knoxville, I received another text message from a casting company asking me to be in NYC in two days so I could be on the HBO show *And Just Like That*, the *Sex In The City* spinoff. Two days later I was calm as I sat in hair and make-up, I felt confident when I met with wardrobe, but when I walked on set and saw Sarah Jessica Parker and Kristin Davis my stomach flipped. My childhood dream was literally happening, and I had the awareness to know I was living it. I was on set all day and even had a run in with some paparazzi. The best part of this entire experience was when I returned home and Halianna looked at me and said the words I will carry in my soul forever, "Mom, I'm so proud of you. You made your dream come true."

The next 45 days were like that. We were in NYC more than we were in Knoxville. We had magical moments on Broadway that year, crying as *Phantom of the Opera* closed after 35 years, holding Red Buckets for Broadway Cares at *The Lion King*, and yes even a backstage visit and photo op with the one and only Aaron Tveit after one of our many visits to the *Moulin Rouge*. As March approached I was happier than I had been in a long time. Work was making money, I had a wonderful team, and we had one more trip to the city with three generations of my family planned over Halianna's spring break.

The trip began with another once-in-a-lifetime experience. We were special guests at Broadway Backwards, a fundraiser hosted by BCEFA. It was like a fairy tale being all dressed up rubbing elbows with some of the greatest talent in the world; and then it happened. The next morning, I woke up before mom and Halianna. When I stood up, I fell to the floor screaming in mind-numbing pain. When I got to the bathroom, I was vomiting from pain.

Looking back, I was incredibly thankful my mom was there because I scared Halianna and I was scared. That trip was just kicking off, and I had spent more money than I was comfortable with making this the trip of a lifetime and it was, but not how I planned. I missed several of the Broadway performances with mom and Halianna because I was in too much pain to make it. I spent three nights in the emergency room in NYC, alone, worried about myself, in gut wrenching pain. The bright spot of the week and of that time was a woman named Stacey Hinkel, who was in charge of my medical health at that time. She was a lifesaver over telehealth, making sure I did not miss every opportunity that week due to pain. I'm going to fast forward a bit to being back in Knoxville. Stacey fought for me because the results of the MRI read that nothing was wrong. Stacey convinced one of the best neurosurgeons in the country to see my case. It turns out the MRI was misread; I have a collapsed disk in my neck that was on top of nerves. Dr. York walked into the exam room in scrubs and cowboy boots with swagger for miles. He was the absolute expert in the room, direct, and confident. He shared, I had three options if this were a normal disk collapse:

1. Treat with physical therapy
2. Move onto pain management if needed
3. Resort to surgery only when necessary

He went on to say, "But your case isn't normal, and I may have unconscious bias toward surgery, but in your case if you do not have neurosurgery within four weeks you could lose the use of your arm." I was at peace because of how Dr. York sold me on the best option. He presented the three options but he was sure of what I needed to do. He was in control of the appointment and was clearly the expert. I underwent neurosurgery three weeks later but the challenging part was yet to come. Dr. York was as good in the operating room as he was in the exam room. I was home the same day of neurosurgery, and recovery began.

A question I'm often asked by students is how to get all the work done needed to run my business when dealing with an illness. Until having neurosurgery I never felt like I had the knowledge to answer that question because I had yet to deal with that specific challenge. Following surgery, I instantly felt better, was out of pain, and I believed I was healed and ready to get to work. But I tried to honor what the neurosurgeon recommended and what my team insisted on by taking at least six weeks off from work. I am sure my body needed rest but nothing about the rest I permitted myself was keeping it super simple. I did not listen to my personal guardrail, I listened to everyone else about what they thought I needed. Meanwhile, I needed to be back at work, I needed to engage with my community, I needed to be on top of all that was going on while I was resting. By the time I returned to work, I was a different person and not in a positive way.

1. In just 90 days, I managed to gain 45 pounds. At this rate, I figured I'd be a heavyweight champion by Christmas!
2. Then the hot flashes started. My thermostat and I had more ups and downs than a soap opera relationship.
3. The brain fog was so intense that some people I was close to actually thought I'd turned into a supervillain. I guess my secret power was forgetting my own name!
4. I learned the fine art of standing outside in the freezing cold just to dodge the dreaded boob sweat and avoid feeling smothered (gross but it's a real problem).
5. And to top it all off, my identity was stolen, along with nearly $150K from my accounts. I guess someone out there really wanted to be me, but with my luck, I should have warned them about the hot flashes and brain fog!
6. I went from being at the top of my game to finding myself post surgery in full blown menopause. There was no easing into it, y'all. One day I was happy, healthy, and hugely successful. The next day hot, hormonal hell wreaked havoc on my life.

As the year ended, I found myself spending every hour of my workday dealing with ID theft instead of selling. My email, social media, banks, credit cards, and more were hacked. I appeared like a completely unorganized flop, missing emails, deadlines, and behavior that was atypical for me. This manuscript was stolen, and I missed so many emails from my publisher that it nearly cost me the book deal. I was unable to access money and ran into difficulty paying my team. My confidence was destroyed. I was too embarrassed to show my face. I'm a fighter but this was the first time in my life I froze. I lost friends who could not find it in their hearts to love me through this time. I lost trust with business colleagues because someone was wreaking destruction on my life. Was this the universe or God telling me it was time to light a match, burn it all down, and start over? That question would haunt me for the next year. Nothing about my business life or personal life was keeping it super simple and the more complicated I allowed things to become, the more both my business and life went sideways.

A.I.D.A

Now, one other thing to keep in mind as we go through the 10 steps for writing a sales page is called AIDA: Attention, Interest, Desire, Action. The Authentic Selling steps are based on AIDA because it's worked since 1898. Yep, 1898! It's the gold standard for a reason.

Writing copy using AIDA is super simple (K.I.S.S. right?):

You have to grab attention.

You have to create interest.

You have to create desire

You have to create action.

So, recognizing your customers' time, K.I.S.S., and AIDA gives you a little bit of a framework for writing copy that converts.

10 Steps for an Authentic Selling® Sales Page

All the steps for your Authentic Selling® Sales Page that converts:

- Step 1: Attention
- Step 2: Interest
- Step 3: Transition to What's Possible
- Step 4: Desire
- Step 5: Transition to Trust
- Step 6: Features + Benefits
- Step 7: Why You Statement
- Step 8: Investment/Call to Action
- Step 9: Buy Me Now Statement
- Step 10: Results/Testimonials

Step 1: Attention

How do you grab your customers' attention? Using either a big bold statement or your Authentic Selling® power statement. The first step of your sales page is that attention-grabbing statement, which is written in paragraph form.

Why Step 1 (Attention) Matters

Authentic Selling® Pro Tip → Step 1 matters because you have eight seconds for Step 1 and Step 2 to get the attention of your potential customers.

> Let's count them.
> One.
> Two.
> Three.
> Four.
> Five.

Six.

Seven.

Eight.

The reason we count them is because that's longer than you think, right? Eight seconds.

You have eight seconds before somebody decides if they want to continue reading after you've got the hook, after you've got their attention, or if they want to go away.

Your customers are in a mode like this: should I stay or should I go now? You have eight seconds to hook them in. Keep that in mind as we build out Step 1 and Step 2 of your authentically written copy.

I'm someone who needs to see it to learn it, so let's follow an example and watch a sales page build. We are going to use an actual sales page that my company used during one of our Authentic Selling® launches. Those launches are typically capped so that I can provide best-in-class service without having my battery dead. This particular year we sold close to a million dollars in sales so this is a sales page that is proven to convert. I'm putting it here as an example of how we create sales pages and teach the creation process so we can follow the same example throughout this process.

Step 1 Example → Attention

You have the life-changing idea, the die-hard commitment, and all the deliverables to make a real difference in the world . . . but if you don't know how to articulate that value to interested buyers your business is broke. Or worse – a very expensive hobby.

Authentic Selling® Note → You may also hear Step 1 called a hook, or trailer, like a movie trailer. I also like to call this a record scratch moment that makes you go "wait, what?"

Step 2: Interest

How do you create interest quickly? You quiz your reader by creating head-nodding copy that actually accomplishes two very important things: It increase conversions and decreases the amount of time it takes to create those conversions.

Why Step 2 Matters

Your customer is either interested and reading your sales page or scrolling and looking at other people's copy. With Step 2 you want to hook them in with your compelling statement that draws attention to the rest of your copy. If you've ever seen a newspaper or magazine article before, the heading (also called hot head) has the exact same purpose, to get the attention of your reader.

Your customers are in a mode like this. Should I stay or should I go now? Your copy has to create interest. You can now use your eight seconds wisely. Eight seconds to hook them in. What are you gonna do with those eight seconds, right? Create interest.

Authentic Selling® Math → Research shows that you need 7–10 silent closes before someone trusts you with their time and money. A silent close is where your potential customer is reading questions on your copy in Step 2 that can only be answered with single word answers, like "yes" or "no."

Think about Step 2 like this; go back to what we know. Your customer is either interested and reading your sales page or scrolling and looking at other people's copy.

When the human brain reads a close-ended question it has a difficult time not answering it, which keeps your potential customers on your page and reading about your offers.

How Do You Create Interest?

This right here is my favorite sales tool among all. I always think of my favorite rapper, Dre, when I teach Step 2. One day I'm gonna meet Dr. Dre and I'm gonna get him to teach this tool in his smooth Dre style and you know what? When Dre teaches one of my sales tools, it's going to be everything, y'all. In 1995 Dr. Dre had a song that talked about "keeping their heads ringin" and that is why I always think of him when I teach this tool, because you want your customers nodding their heads yes to the Step 2 part of your sales copy.

To really hook your customers with Step 2, you want to show the reader that you've got something that they need to hear, right. Creating interest is the way to keep them hooked after Step 1 and you've grabbed attention.

Step 2 is best done by quizzing the reader using the questions below.

Do you?

Have you?

Are you?

Those questions are followed by a pain point from your Authentic Selling® Sales Map. Think of this step as rapid fire, bullet, bullet, bullet.

Create the Interest Bullets of Your Sales Page

Option 1 Do you	Option 2 Have you	Option 3 Are you
• Insert pain point 1	Insert pain point 1	Insert pain point 1
• Insert pain point 2	Insert pain point 2	Insert pain point 2
• Insert pain point 3	Insert pain point 3	Insert pain point 3

- Do you want more happiness in your life? Automatically, your brain is going to head nod and say, "yep, of course I do!"
- Do you want more laughter in your life? Your brain will head nod and say "Yes!"
- Do you want_____? Your brain will head nod and say yes.

Example Sales Page

Attention

You have the life-changing idea, the die-hard commitment, and all the deliverables to make a real difference in the world . . . but if you don't know how to articulate that value to interested buyers your business is broke. Or worse – a very expensive hobby.

Interest

- Hustling harder and harder, month after month, and STILL not cracking $50K in revenue?
- Sinking more and more money into your business and not seeing ANY returns?
- Wasting valuable time on free consult calls that always seem to end with potential clients going missing in action (MIA) (or courting your competitors; ugh)?

- Telling yourself – "I just CAN'T do sales!" . . .
- Sitting on a sales call palms sweating, trying desperately not to sound, well . . . desperate?
- Wondering if potential customers can tell you're new at this?
- Pricing your offers wrong and thinking it's probably not even worth that much?
- Throwing in extras is the only way you can seal the deal?
- End your day feeling like more of a fraud than an expert?

You're ready to give up. You just don't have what it takes to do this. You're missing that killer, eye-of-the-tiger, take 'em down at all costs, predatory drive that you need to make the sale.

When you add those into your sales page you are using a sales process called a **silent close**. They're micro silent closes, but sales research shows it takes about 7 to 10 closes before somebody trusts you to give you their hard-earned money and their precious time.

Paragraphs vs. Bullets

Authentic Selling® Truth → Very rarely do people read an entire sales page, which is kind of disheartening because think about all the work that we put into creating sales pages. The truth is people skim, so that means copy that sells is scannable copy. Your readers are looking for the benefits of what you offer. Remember people buy off of emotion and justify with logic. You want them to be able to skim your copy super easily, especially on a phone. If your copy is long – paragraph after paragraph after paragraph – people are going to be like, oh my god, bored now, bored now, bored now, and they are on to the next thing.

Step 3: Transition to What's Possible

Step 3 is done in super small, one to two sentences. This transition is taking your customer from the land of pain, because that's where we just were with Steps 1 and 2, to the land of possibility. This is really about dreaming, and we're going to go into more than that in just a moment. A word that works well when you create your transition is "imagine."

Imagine how it will feel when you close your first sale, your first $10K month, $50K month, or even your first million dollars.

That's all you do in Step 3; easy, right?

Example Sales Page

Attention

You have the life-changing idea, the die-hard commitment, and all the deliverables to make a real difference in the world . . . but if you don't know how to articulate that value to interested buyers your business is broke. Or worse – a very expensive hobby.

Interest

- Hustling harder and harder, month after month, and STILL not cracking $50K in revenue?
- Sinking more and more money into your business and not seeing ANY returns?
- Wasting valuable time on free consult calls that always seem to end with potential clients going missing in action (MIA) (or courting your competitors; ugh)?
- Telling yourself – "I just CAN'T do sales!" . . .
- Sitting on a sales call palms sweating, trying desperately not to sound, well . . . desperate?
- Wondering if potential customers can tell you're new at this?
- Pricing your offers wrong and thinking it's probably not even worth that much?
- Throwing in extras is the only way you can seal the deal?
- End your day feeling like more of a fraud than an expert?

You're ready to give up. You just don't have what it takes to do this. You're missing that killer, eye-of-the-tiger, take 'em down at all costs, predatory drive that you need to make the sale.

Transition to What's Possible

Imagine how it will feel when you close your first sale, your first $10K month, $50K month, or even your first million dollars.

Step 4: Desire

How Do You Create Desire?

It's time to really create a strong sense of desire to change your customers' lives. You need to create three to five bullet points in this step where you bring the attention back to what your ideal customer is dreaming is possible as it relates to what you're selling. We're simply talking about the land of desire and the goal is to get the reader dreaming in this step. What would it feel like to . . . [insert a benefit, imagine, again imagine]? How different would it be if you insert a benefit straight from your Sales Map? Can you see why your Sales Map is so important? It shortcuts time and creates incredible copy that sells.

Now keeping in mind that sellable copy is scannable copy and in Step 3, transition to what's possible, we had a couple of sentences. What format does that mean Step 4 is going to be in? Bullet points, right?

Creating desire is important because this is where your potential customers begin to dream about what's possible for them and how what you're offering them could help them get what they want.

Authentic Selling Truth → You don't want to make claims that seem so outrageous that it's impossible to deliver; instead, these claims need to be related to your products and services. You can use your benefits tools from Chapter 4 to do that. Step 4 is basically where you're going to insert some benefits from your Sales Map.

Remember in Step 4 you haven't promised anything yet, but you're getting ready to talk about the difference that your product or service makes.

Authentic Selling® Pro Tip → A great way to get customer language also is to look back at testimonials. If you have past testimonials, then you can insert items here into this desired statement. We really want people to begin to get a taste of what is possible when they interact with your brand or your business.

Authentic Selling® Pro Tip → Now, this is not a promise of what your product or service will do. Step 4 is only getting the customer to think about how their lives could be different after using your product or service.

Examples of Step 4

- What if your next launch was your biggest launch yet?
- What if you tripled what you made last year?
- What if you were able to take that vacation that you and your family have always dreamed of taking?
- How amazing would you feel if you won the lottery?

Example Sales Page

Attention

You have the life-changing idea, the die-hard commitment, and all the deliverables to make a real difference in the world . . . but if you don't know how to articulate that value to interested buyers your business is broke. Or worse – a very expensive hobby.

Interest

- Hustling harder and harder, month after month, and STILL not cracking $50K in revenue?
- Sinking more and more money into your business and not seeing ANY returns?
- Wasting valuable time on free consult calls that always seem to end with potential clients going missing in action (MIA) (or courting your competitors; ugh)?
- Telling yourself – "I just CAN'T do sales!" . . .
- Sitting on a sales call palms sweating, trying desperately not to sound, well . . . desperate?
- Wondering if potential customers can tell you're new at this?
- Pricing your offers wrong and thinking it's probably not even worth that much?

Your Authentically Written Sales Page Copy

- Throwing in some extras is the only way you can seal the deal?
- End your day feeling like more of a fraud than an expert?

You're ready to give up. You just don't have what it takes to do this. You're missing that killer, eye-of-the-tiger, take 'em down at all costs, predatory drive that you need to make the sale.

Transition to What's Possible

Imagine how it will feel when you close your first sale, your first $10K month, $50K month, or even your first million dollars.

Desire

- Learn how to sell with calm, unshakeable confidence (no more sweaty palms or self-doubt spirals).
- Effortlessly build loyal, long-lasting customer relationships (i.e. RAVING fans) – so you never have to worry about losing out to the competition.
- Handle objections with class and charm like a well-seasoned pro, and hear "YES!" on the regular.
- Consistently close sales in a way that feels like you're helping a friend – not harassing a stranger.
- End your sales calls with your customer BEGGING to work with you and handing over their credit card number! (They'll even thank YOU for the opportunity!)
- Be EXCITED to get on the phone with prospects, because you know how to have easy, engaging, and feel-good conversations that convert into clients – and big bucks.
- Have the confidence to create compelling, premium offers that you KNOW are worth every penny – so you can work smarter, not harder, and finally make the money you need to have the freedom you want.
- Generate major buzz on social media about your services and products that lead to month-long wait lists, sold-out masterminds, and five-figure launches.

Step 5: Transition to Trust

Transitioning to trust is a very important piece of the process. You create another transition. It's called Transition to Trust and it is a little bit longer than bullets. In this section you are back to writing sentences, not bullet points. We're going to break this sentence down into multiple steps.

- Step 1 in creating Transition to Trust sentences → Compliment them.

Example of sentence number 1 as you transition to trust:

- You're a brilliant business owner on a mission to improve the lives of your customers
- A mama who's doing it all.
- A woman who is walking backward in high heels trying to make sure that everything gets done for everybody.
- Whether you're a direct sales rising star or you run your own online modern business.

You're simply putting some customer identifiers here so that customers can self-identify you are talking about them.

- Step 2 in creating a Transition to Trust sentence → Introduce your product or service.

Example of second step sentence as you create Transition to Trust:
"That's the exact reason I created _____ [insert the name of your product or service] to take you From_____ [insert the pain point from your Authentic Selling® Sales Map]

- Step 3 in creating Transition to Trust sentence → Show your customer what is possible when they buy what you're selling.

Example of third step sentence as you create Transition to Trust:
"That's the exact reason I created _____ [insert the name of your product or service] to take you From_____ [pain point from your Authentic Selling® Sales Map] To_____ [benefit from Authentic Selling® Sales Map]

Let's see this in full action here in the Transition to Trust sentence examples.

"You are a mama who's walking backward in high heels on tightropes every day. You juggle all the schedules, all the food, getting the kids to where they need to go, but you need a break. That's the exact reason I created Live More Now: to take you from running your life looking like a Marge Simpson to sashaying through life with grace, ease, and possibility like Audrey Hepburn."

"You are a corporate executive who needs to be able to get in touch with his team immediately. Your current cell phone plan is dropping calls more than basketball players drop balls."

Another way you can transition to trust is to create a hole that your customer needs to fill and your product or service is the thing that fills the hole.

Here's how it works when your customer has this problem.

Other words you can use in your Transition to Trust statement are listed below.

- You need _____
- You're missing _____
- You're stuck _____
- You deserve _____
- You're looking for_____

Example Sales Page

Attention

You have the life-changing idea, the die-hard commitment, and all the deliverables to make a real difference in the world . . . but if you don't know how to articulate that value to interested buyers your business is broke. Or worse – a very expensive hobby.

Interest

- Hustling harder and harder, month after month, and STILL not cracking $50K in revenue?

- Sinking more and more money into your business and not seeing ANY returns?
- Wasting valuable time on free consult calls that always seem to end with potential clients going missing in action (MIA) (or courting your competitors; ugh)?
- Telling yourself – "I just CAN'T do sales!" . . .
- Sitting on a sales call palms sweating, trying desperately not to sound, well . . . desperate?
- Wondering if potential customers can tell you're new at this?
- Pricing your offers wrong and thinking it's probably not even worth that much?
- Throwing in some extras is the only way you can seal the deal?
- End your day feeling like more of a fraud than an expert?

You're ready to give up. You just don't have what it takes to do this. You're missing that killer, eye-of-the-tiger, take 'em down at all costs, predatory drive that you need to make the sale.

Transition to What's Possible
Imagine how it will feel when you close your first sale, your first $10K month, $50K month, or even your first million dollars.

Desire
- Learn how to sell with calm, unshakeable confidence (no more sweaty palms or self-doubt spirals).
- Effortlessly build loyal, long-lasting customer relationships (i.e. RAVING fans) – so you never have to worry about losing out to the competition.
- Handle objections with class and charm like a well-seasoned pro, and hear "YES!" on the regular.
- Consistently close sales in a way that feels like you're helping a friend – not harassing a stranger.

- End your sales calls with your customer BEGGING to work with you and handing over their credit card number! (They'll even thank YOU for the opportunity!)
- Be EXCITED to get on the phone with prospects, because you know how to have easy, engaging, and feel-good conversations that convert into clients – and big bucks.
- Have the confidence to create compelling, premium offers that you KNOW are worth every penny – so you can work smarter, not harder, and finally make the money you need to have the freedom you want.
- Generate major buzz on social media about your services and products that lead to month-long wait lists, sold-out masterminds, and five-figure launches.

Transition to Trust

Sales School was created for people just like you – honest business owners who want an ick-free, easily repeatable, step-by-step process for selling so you can make more money and a bigger difference without selling your soul.

You may not be able to see it right now but I can! I've lived it! I've taught more than 1,000 other students in 186 countries who have lived it, and I want you to live it, too!

You deserve a business that makes you money.

So if what you've been doing isn't working . . .

(and you've got the bank statements to prove it) . . .

You've got a sales problem. The good news is – learning to sell isn't rocket science!

Step 6: Features + Benefits

What Are Features + Benefits?

This is what most people think of when they think of sales copy; it's the what's included section, or as I call it, the how are you going to accomplish these promises you're making. It's also where you promise what your product can do.

Let's go back for a second, if you remember when we were creating your Sales Map, I told you features do not sell, but we've been taught to just throw all the features in. Facebook groups, unlimited email access, 40 million calls, homework, feedback. Oh my gosh! I don't want all that stuff. **I want the results.**

So your new rule for this step of your sales page is do not have a feature without a benefit. That's it. They are like strawberries and champagne, peanut butter and chocolate, green beans and carrots. Kendrick and good shoes. Features + benefits just go together. Period. You don't have a feature without a benefit; I can't stress that enough. These steps are where we really take control of the process and start selling. This is where we tell people what they're going to get for their investment.

Grab your completed Sales Map.

Bullet your features + benefits.

- How is the offer delivered + why does this matter
- What's included in the offer + why does this matter
- Anything else that is included with the offer + why does this matter
- Just a benefit
- Just a benefit

Why Do Features and Benefits Matter?

Authentic Selling® Real Talk → Nobody wants to learn how to have sales calls. When you put your head on your pillow at night, are you dreaming of sales calls? No, you want to know **how to close customers, make money, do more of what you love, create financial freedom. Those are your benefits.**

Authentic Selling® Pro Tip → Features and benefits are not all going to be written the same because everybody's products and services are different. If your product or service is broken down by weeks after you do these bullet points of features plus benefits, you can go into the breakdown.

Optional Step Breakdown Week by Week Features (Optional)

Option 1

Week 1, you will learn to_____ [insert benefit].

Week 2 allows you to_____ [insert benefit].

Option 2

At the conclusion of week 2, you will be able to _____ [insert benefit].

As a result of the _____ [insert feature] you learn in week 3, you will create _____ [insert benefit].

Features + Benefits

Welcome to Sales School, the #1 sales training for your business.

Sales School is a seven-week interactive program backed by high-touch expert coaching, results-driven training, and long-term support like nothing else out there.

The step-by-step process we teach will help you feel amazingly confident selling your products and services. You will learn the proven sales tools, systems, and strategies you've been missing, so you can attract loyal customers through genuine engagement and overcome objections with grace.

So that you can actually DO the work you're meant to do (AND make a living doing it).

Your business will make more money without you needing to be a sales bully.

- Sales School will provide you the tools to go from struggling to find your customers to actually doing the work you're meant to do (AND make a living doing it).

- You'll go from feeling like you've tried everything when it comes to marketing but nothing's working to making more money without you needing to be a sales bully.

- Built a big, beautiful business model but still can't manage to build a big, beautiful bank account? Learn to convert 50% more potential customers by mastering your follow-ups and turning a "maybe" into "where do I sign!"

Whether you're trying to land your first paying client or trying to hit the 100K mark, Sales School provides you with proven sales tools, systems, and strategies you've been missing, so you can attract loyal customers through genuine engagement and overcome objections with grace.

Example Sales Page

Attention

You have the life-changing idea, the die-hard commitment, and all the deliverables to make a real difference in the world . . . but if you don't know how to articulate that value to interested buyers your business is broke. Or worse – a very expensive hobby.

Interest

- Hustling harder and harder, month after month, and STILL not cracking $50K in revenue?
- Sinking more and more money into your business and not seeing ANY returns?
- Wasting valuable time on free consult calls that always seem to end with potential clients going missing in action (MIA) (or courting your competitors; ugh)?
- Telling yourself – "I just CAN'T do sales!" . . .
- Sitting on a sales call palms sweating, trying desperately not to sound, well . . . desperate?
- Wondering if potential customers can tell you're new at this?
- Pricing your offers wrong and thinking it's probably not even worth that much?
- Throwing in some extras is the only way you can seal the deal?
- End your day feeling like more of a fraud than an expert?

You're ready to give up. You just don't have what it takes to do this. You're missing that killer, eye-of-the-tiger, take 'em down at all costs, predatory drive that you need to make the sale.

Transition to What's Possible
Imagine how it will feel when you close your first sale, your first $10K month, $50K month, or even your first million dollars.

Desire
- Learn how to sell with calm, unshakeable confidence (no more sweaty palms or self-doubt spirals).
- Effortlessly build loyal, long-lasting customer relationships (i.e. RAVING fans) – so you never have to worry about losing out to the competition.
- Handle objections with class and charm like a well-seasoned pro, and hear "YES!" on the regular.
- Consistently close sales in a way that feels like you're helping a friend – not harassing a stranger.
- End your sales calls with your customer BEGGING to work with you and handing over their credit card number! (They'll even thank YOU for the opportunity!)
- Be EXCITED to get on the phone with prospects, because you know how to have easy, engaging, and feel-good conversations that convert into clients – and big bucks.
- Have the confidence to create compelling, premium offers that you KNOW are worth every penny – so you can work smarter, not harder, and finally make the money you need to have the freedom you want.
- Generate major buzz on social media about your services and products that lead to month-long wait lists, sold-out masterminds, and five-figure launches.

Transition to Trust
Sales School was created for people just like you – honest business owners who want an ick-free, easily repeatable, step-by-step process for selling so you can make more money and a bigger difference without selling your soul.

You may not be able to see it right now but I can! I've lived it! I've taught more than 1,000 other students in 186 countries who have lived it, and I want you to live it, too!

You deserve a business that makes you money.

So if what you've been doing isn't working . . .

(and you've got the bank statements to prove it) . . .

You've got a sales problem. The good news is – learning to sell isn't rocket science!

Features + Benefits

Welcome to Sales School, the #1 sales training for your business.

Sales School is a seven-week interactive program backed by high-touch expert coaching, results-driven training, and long-term support like nothing else out there.

The step-by-step process we teach will help you feel amazingly confident selling your products and services. You will learn the proven sales tools, systems, and strategies you've been missing, so you can attract loyal customers through genuine engagement and overcome objections with grace.

So that you can actually DO the work you're meant to do (AND make a living doing it).

Your business will make more money without you needing to be a sales bully.

- Sales School will provide you the tools to go from struggling to find your customers to actually doing the work you're meant to do (AND make a living doing it).
- You'll go from feeling like you've tried everything when it comes to marketing but nothing's working to making more money without you needing to be a sales bully.
- Built a big, beautiful business model but still can't manage to build a big, beautiful bank account? Learn to convert 50% more potential customers by mastering your follow-ups and turning a "maybe" into "where do I sign!"

Whether you're trying to land your first paying client or trying to hit the 100K mark, Sales School provides you with proven sales tools, systems, and strategies you've been missing, so you can attract loyal customers through genuine engagement and overcome objections with grace.

Step 7: Why You Statement

What is a "why you" statement? It is as self-explanatory as it sounds. This step is where you get to tell your audience why they can trust you to deliver all that you promise. This needs to be emotional copy. It needs to be copy that speaks to your customers. After all, people buy off of emotion and justify with logic, right? What that means is your customers buy off of benefits and justify with features. Get in the mindset of what they're going to get, or what makes you or your offer, your class, your product so flipping amazing. It can be one sentence, it can be three to five sentences, but this is your Why You Statement.

> **Example of Why You Statement**
> "What makes working with Jasmine so amazing is_____,"
> "What makes life coaching with me different is _____."

Why the "Why You" Statement Matters

Authentic Selling® Pro Tip → You need to know why somebody is going to choose you over somebody else. You may be saying, I don't have competition, I don't like this. Great! Then don't consider it competition. But if people are going to give you their money and their time, you need to know why. You need to know what attracts them to you, what is attractive about your offer to them. So, for example, what makes Authentic Selling unlike anything else out there is the number one sales training for your modern business. It has been taken by thousands of students on five continents. All of whom have used it to improve their business to get more customers, make more money, do more of what they love.

It could be that, if you're just getting started, you could maybe use a testimonial here. Customers say that working with Susie is unlike anything else because of how she marries the emotional with the physical. And that creates a unique experience that allows us to get to the root of the problem and solve it so that you have more light, laughter, happiness in your life. Your copy here needs to be on point. Think about what makes you unique. Maybe it's that you're "sweet as pie, tough as nails," which Laura Belgray says about me.

Another example is "Kendrick has been nicknamed the most over delivering woman online by her students, which means that you are never going to be left alone to figure it out. You're going to have the tools you need to do more of what you love, make more money, get more customers, create financial freedom."

Authentic Selling® Pro Tip → This isn't the place to tell your story. Even if your story is relevant, it goes on an "About" page. Your sales page is all about what you can do for your customers.

List 1–3 accomplishments.

- What training do you have?
- How long have you been studying this information?
- Where did you get certified?
- How does any of this help your customer?
- Other

Brainstorm why someone would choose your business to help them solve their problem, also known as Your Big Freaking Deal Statement (BFD)

- Training?
- Years of experience?
- The number of people you've worked with?
- Customer testimonial?

Example Option 1

What makes working with _____ [insert business name] unlike others is _____ [insert BFD statement].

Your Authentically Written Sales Page Copy

Example Option 2

[Insert company name] is committed to _____, which means _____ [insert how this helps customers].

Example Option 3

Our customers like results, and we are a results kind of business.

Example Sales Page

Attention

You have the life-changing idea, the die-hard commitment, and all the deliverables to make a real difference in the world . . . but if you don't know how to articulate that value to interested buyers your business is broke. Or worse – a very expensive hobby.

Interest

- Hustling harder and harder, month after month, and STILL not cracking $50K in revenue?
- Sinking more and more money into your business and not seeing ANY returns?
- Wasting valuable time on free consult calls that always seem to end with potential clients going missing in action (MIA) (or courting your competitors; ugh)?
- Telling yourself – "I just CAN'T do sales!" . . .
- Sitting on a sales call palms sweating, trying desperately not to sound, well . . . desperate?
- Wondering if potential customers can tell you're new at this?
- Pricing your offers wrong and thinking it's probably not even worth that much?
- Throwing in some extras is the only way you can seal the deal?
- End your day feeling like more of a fraud than an expert?

You're ready to give up. You just don't have what it takes to do this. You're missing that killer, eye-of-the-tiger, take 'em down at all costs, predatory drive that you need to make the sale.

Transition to What's Possible

Imagine how it will feel when you close your first sale, your first $10K month, $50K month, or even your first million dollars.

Desire

- Learn how to sell with calm, unshakeable confidence (no more sweaty palms or self-doubt spirals).
- Effortlessly build loyal, long-lasting customer relationships (i.e. RAVING fans) – so you never have to worry about losing out to the competition.
- Handle objections with class and charm like a well-seasoned pro, and hear "YES!" on the regular.
- Consistently close sales in a way that feels like you're helping a friend – not harassing a stranger.
- End your sales calls with your customer BEGGING to work with you and handing over their credit card number! (They'll even thank YOU for the opportunity!)
- Be EXCITED to get on the phone with prospects, because you know how to have easy, engaging, and feel-good conversations that convert into clients – and big bucks.
- Have the confidence to create compelling, premium offers that you KNOW are worth every penny – so you can work smarter, not harder, and finally make the money you need to have the freedom you want.
- Generate major buzz on social media about your services and products that lead to month-long wait lists, sold-out masterminds, and five-figure launches.

Transition to Trust

You can do ALL that while still being your authentic, helpful, genuine, brilliant, charming self. You CAN find your customers, share your products and services, AND create raving fans like the real, connected, heart-centered person and change-maker that you actually are. The whole "won't take no for an answer" way of making sales is old and outdated. More importantly, people are tired of it.

Features + Benefits

Welcome to Sales School, the #1 sales training for your business.

Sales School is a seven-week interactive program backed by high-touch expert coaching, results-driven training, and long-term support like nothing else out there.

The step-by-step process we teach will help you feel amazingly confident selling your products and services. You will learn the proven sales tools, systems, and strategies you've been missing, so you can attract loyal customers through genuine engagement and overcome objections with grace.

So that you can actually DO the work you're meant to do (AND make a living doing it).

Your business will make more money without you needing to be a sales bully.

- Sales School will provide you the tools to go from struggling to find your customers to actually doing the work you're meant to do (AND make a living doing it).
- You'll go from feeling like you've tried everything when it comes to marketing but nothing's working to making more money without you needing to be a sales bully.
- Built a big, beautiful business model but still can't manage to build a big, beautiful bank account? Learn to convert 50% more potential customers by mastering your follow-ups and turning a "maybe" into "where do I sign!"

Whether you're trying to land your first paying client or trying to hit the 100K mark, Sales School provides you with proven sales tools, systems, and strategies you've been missing, so you can attract loyal customers through genuine engagement and overcome objections with grace.

Why You Statement

Sales School was created for people just like you – honest business owners who want an ick-free, easily repeatable, step-by-step process for selling so you can make more money and a bigger difference without selling your soul.

You may not be able to see it right now but I can! I've lived it! I've taught more than 1,000 other students in 186 countries who have lived it, and I want you to live it, too!

You deserve a business that makes you money.

So if what you've been doing isn't working . . .

(and you've got the bank statements to prove it) . . .

You've got a sales problem. The good news is – learning to sell isn't rocket science!

Today, I'm one of the top sales coaches in the business – and I'm KNOWN for getting results.

Step 8: Investment/Call to Action (CTA)

What is the Investment/CTA? This section is where you share the investment, how much money and time it will cost to get access to your product or service.

Authentic Selling® Pro Tip → Don't shy away from the investment. The investment is what it is and that's why the "Why You Statement" is so important.

Should you put your prices on your website? There are countless opinions on this. Here's my approach for Authentic Selling®, though it's not a hard and fast rule. Some things are absolute, like the definition of selling is "the exchange of money for a product or service." That's not a Kendrickism; it's the black-and-white truth.

What you're about to learn **is** a Kendrickism.

Should You Put Your Prices on Your Website?

When possible, yes, put the price on the website. However, there are times when it's not beneficial to share prices on your website. In the past, as I grew this business, I became comfortable investing in myself. I've spent $50,000 on a mastermind to hit $1 million in business. At the time, I wasn't keen on broadcasting how much I'd spent. If the prices had been on the coach's website, it might have deterred me. So, think about your customers.

I have experiences through Authentic Selling® that cost $25,000–$40,000. We don't list these prices online, not to bait and switch, but out of respect for those who pay them.

Authentic Selling Pro Tip → Our rule at Authentic Selling® is that if it's under $10,000, we put the price on the website. If it's more than $10,000, we don't. This isn't a black-and-white rule; you need to find what works for your business. Consider if your customers are comfortable with others knowing what they paid.

When listing the investment, be straightforward. Different calls to action can include "Buy now," "Fill out an application," or "Schedule a sales call."

1. If it's a buy now option, list payment plans.
2. Don't make the font tiny because you're embarrassed about the price.

Own your worth. The investment is what it is. Your next step is to get the call to action on the page. We have a resource of ready-made calls to action for you. Whether it's "Buy now," "Fill out an application," or "Schedule a call."

Examples of Calls to Action

1. Start your free trial today.
2. Try it free.
3. Get started.
4. Your next step to health begins here.
5. Your baby's sleep begins today.
6. Making money in your business starts here.
7. Learn more.

8. Learn how, here. It's free.
9. Get started with your healthier lifestyle today.
10. A healthier lifestyle starts here.
11. Experience the difference.
12. **Next Steps**

    Enroll OR

    Have questions? Wonder if this is the right step for you?

    Email authenticselling@kendrickshope.com to get your questions answered.
13. **Next Steps**

    Fill out the application here.

    You will be contacted within 24 hours to schedule a no-obligation sales chat.

    Taking control of your business sales has never been so fun.

    Let's get started.
14. **Next Step**

    Schedule your no-obligation consult here.

    Taking control of your business sales has never been so fun.

    Let's get started.

Create Your Call to Action

Option 1

1. The investment is _____.
2. Insert "Buy Now Statement."

Option 2

1. Have questions? Wonder if this is the right step for you?
2. Email _____ [insert email] to get your questions answered.
3. Insert "Buy Now Statement."

Your Authentically Written Sales Page Copy

Option 3
1. Next Steps
2. Fill out the application here.
3. You will be contacted within 24 hours to schedule a no-obligation sales chat.
4. Insert "Buy Now Statement."

Example Sales Page

Attention

You have the life-changing idea, the die-hard commitment, and all the deliverables to make a real difference in the world . . . but if you don't know how to articulate that value to interested buyers your business is broke. Or worse – a very expensive hobby.

Interest

- Hustling harder and harder, month after month, and STILL not cracking $50K in revenue?
- Sinking more and more money into your business and not seeing ANY returns?
- Wasting valuable time on free consult calls that always seem to end with potential clients going missing in action (MIA) (or courting your competitors; ugh)?
- Telling yourself – "I just CAN'T do sales!" . . .
- Sitting on a sales call palms sweating, trying desperately not to sound, well . . . desperate?
- Wondering if potential customers can tell you're new at this?
- Pricing your offers wrong and thinking it's probably not even worth that much?
- Throwing in some extras is the only way you can seal the deal?
- End your day feeling like more of a fraud than an expert?

You're ready to give up. You just don't have what it takes to do this. You're missing that killer, eye-of-the-tiger, take 'em down at all costs, predatory drive that you need to make the sale.

Transition to What's Possible

Imagine how it will feel when you close your first sale, your first $10K month, $50K month, or even your first million dollars.

Desire

- Learn how to sell with calm, unshakeable confidence (no more sweaty palms or self-doubt spirals).
- Effortlessly build loyal, long-lasting customer relationships (i.e. RAVING fans) – so you never have to worry about losing out to the competition.
- Handle objections with class and charm like a well-seasoned pro, and hear "YES!" on the regular.
- Consistently close sales in a way that feels like you're helping a friend – not harassing a stranger.
- End your sales calls with your customer BEGGING to work with you and handing over their credit card number! (They'll even thank YOU for the opportunity!)
- Be EXCITED to get on the phone with prospects, because you know how to have easy, engaging, and feel-good conversations that convert into clients – and big bucks.
- Have the confidence to create compelling, premium offers that you KNOW are worth every penny – so you can work smarter, not harder, and finally make the money you need to have the freedom you want.
- Generate major buzz on social media about your services and products that lead to month-long wait lists, sold-out masterminds, and five-figure launches.

Transition to Trust

You can do ALL that while still being your authentic, helpful, genuine, brilliant, charming self. You CAN find your customers, share your products and services, AND create raving fans like the real, connected, heart-centered person and change-maker that you actually are. The whole "won't take no for an answer" way of making sales is old and outdated. More importantly, people are tired of it.

Features + Benefits

Welcome to Sales School, the #1 sales training for your business.

Sales School is a seven-week interactive program backed by high-touch expert coaching, results-driven training, and long-term support like nothing else out there.

The step-by-step process we teach will help you feel amazingly confident selling your products and services. You will learn the proven sales tools, systems, and strategies you've been missing, so you can attract loyal customers through genuine engagement and overcome objections with grace.

So that you can actually DO the work you're meant to do (AND make a living doing it).

Your business will make more money without you needing to be a sales bully.

- Sales School will provide you the tools to go from struggling to find your customers to actually doing the work you're meant to do (AND make a living doing it).
- You'll go from feeling like you've tried everything when it comes to marketing but nothing's working to making more money without you needing to be a sales bully.
- Built a big, beautiful business model but still can't manage to build a big, beautiful bank account? Learn to convert 50% more potential customers by mastering your follow-ups and turning a "maybe" into "where do I sign!"

Whether you're trying to land your first paying client or trying to hit the 100K mark, Sales School provides you with proven sales tools, systems, and strategies you've been missing, so you can attract loyal customers through genuine engagement and overcome objections with grace.

Why You Statement

Sales School was created for people just like you – honest business owners who want an ick-free, easily repeatable, step-by-step process for selling so you can make more money and a bigger difference without selling your soul.

You may not be able to see it right now but I can! I've lived it! I've taught more than 1,000 other students in 186 countries who have lived it and I want you to live it, too!

You Deserve a Business That Makes You Money.

So if what you've been doing isn't working . . .

(and you've got the bank statements to prove it) . . .

You've got a sales problem. The good news is – learning to sell isn't rocket science!

Today, I'm one of the top sales coaches in the business – and I'm KNOWN for getting results.

Investment/Call to Action

Choose the Authentic Selling® University Plan That Works Best for You

One Payment of	Four Monthly Payments of	Ten Monthly Payments of
$4,000 USD	$1,000 USD	$400 USD
Join now	Join now	Join now

Ready to shortcut years of trying to figure out sales skills on your own by trial and error? Learn proven strategies to make sales with empathy and get real support from a sales expert every step of the way. Sales School is waiting for you.

Step 9: Buy Me Now Statement

What is a buy me now statement? Your "Buy Me Now" statement basically goes at the end of your investment and this statement is full of benefits. It's the one thing you want them to know that convinces them to buy. It's as simple as that.

Examples of Buy Me Now Statement

Taking control of _____ [insert benefit] has never been so fun.

Example Sales Page

Attention

You have the life-changing idea, the die-hard commitment, and all the deliverables to make a real difference in the world . . . but if you don't know how to articulate that value to interested buyers your business is broke. Or worse – a very expensive hobby.

Interest

- Hustling harder and harder, month after month, and STILL not cracking $50K in revenue?
- Sinking more and more money into your business and not seeing ANY returns?
- Wasting valuable time on free consult calls that always seem to end with potential clients going missing in action (MIA) (or courting your competitors; ugh)?
- Telling yourself – "I just CAN'T do sales!" . . .
- Sitting on a sales call palms sweating, trying desperately not to sound, well . . . desperate?
- Wondering if potential customers can tell you're new at this?
- Pricing your offers wrong and thinking it's probably not even worth that much?
- Throwing in some extras is the only way you can seal the deal?
- End your day feeling like more of a fraud than an expert?

You're ready to give up. You just don't have what it takes to do this. You're missing that killer, eye-of-the-tiger, take 'em down at all costs, predatory drive that you need to make the sale.

Transition to What's Possible

Imagine how it will feel when you close your first sale, your first $10K month, $50K month, or even your first million dollars.

Desire
- Learn how to sell with calm, unshakeable confidence (no more sweaty palms or self-doubt spirals).
- Effortlessly build loyal, long-lasting customer relationships (i.e. RAVING fans) – so you never have to worry about losing out to the competition.
- Handle objections with class and charm like a well-seasoned pro, and hear "YES!" on the regular.
- Consistently close sales in a way that feels like you're helping a friend – not harassing a stranger.
- End your sales calls with your customer BEGGING to work with you and handing over their credit card number! (They'll even thank YOU for the opportunity!)
- Be EXCITED to get on the phone with prospects, because you know how to have easy, engaging, and feel-good conversations that convert into clients – and big bucks.
- Have the confidence to create compelling, premium offers that you KNOW are worth every penny – so you can work smarter, not harder, and finally make the money you need to have the freedom you want.
- Generate major buzz on social media about your services and products that lead to month-long wait lists, sold-out masterminds, and five-figure launches.

Transition to Trust
You can do ALL that while still being your authentic, helpful, genuine, brilliant, charming self. You CAN find your customers, share your products and services, AND create raving fans like the real, connected, heart-centered person and change-maker that you actually are. The whole "won't take no for an answer" way of making sales is old and outdated. More importantly, people are tired of it.

Features + Benefits
Welcome to Sales School, the #1 sales training for your business

Sales School is a seven-week interactive program backed by high-touch expert coaching, results-driven training, and long-term support like nothing else out there.

The step-by-step process we teach will help you feel amazingly confident selling your products and services. You will learn the proven sales tools, systems, and strategies you've been missing, so you can attract loyal customers through genuine engagement and overcome objections with grace.

So that you can actually DO the work you're meant to do (AND make a living doing it).

Your business will make more money without you needing to be a sales bully.

- Sales School will provide you the tools to go from struggling to find your customers to actually doing the work you're meant to do (AND make a living doing it).
- You'll go from feeling like you've tried everything when it comes to marketing but nothing's working to making more money without you needing to be a sales bully.
- Built a big, beautiful business model but still can't manage to build a big, beautiful bank account? Learn to convert 50% more potential customers by mastering your follow-ups and turning a "maybe" into "where do I sign!"

Whether you're trying to land your first paying client or trying to hit the 100K mark, Sales School provides you with proven sales tools, systems, and strategies you've been missing, so you can attract loyal customers through genuine engagement and overcome objections with grace.

Why You Statement

Sales School was created for people just like you – honest business owners who want an ick-free, easily repeatable, step-by-step process for selling so you can make more money and a bigger difference without selling your soul.

You may not be able to see it right now but I can! I've lived it! I've taught more than 1,000 other students in 186 countries who have lived it, and I want you to live it, too!

You Deserve a Business That Makes You Money.

So if what you've been doing isn't working . . .

(and you've got the bank statements to prove it) . . .

You've got a sales problem. The good news is – learning to sell isn't rocket science!

Today, I'm one of the top sales coaches in the business – and I'm KNOWN for getting results.

Investment/Call to Action

Choose the Authentic Selling® University Plan That Works Best for You

One Payment of	Four Monthly Payments of	Ten Monthly Payments of
$4,000	$1,000	$400
USD	USD	USD
Join now	Join now	Join now

Ready to shortcut years of trying to figure out sales skills on your own by trial and error? Learn proven strategies to make sales with empathy and get real support from a sales expert every step of the way. Sales School is waiting for you.

Buy Me Now Statement

Ready to shortcut years of trying to figure out sales skills on your own by trial and error? Learn proven strategies to make sales with empathy and get real support from a sales expert every step of the way. Sales School is waiting for you.

Each semester is limited to 100 students only to make sure you get the attention you deserve.

Step 10: Results/Testimonials

Create trust by inserting testimonials from past clients; but what if you do not have testimonials?

Authentic Selling® Pro Tip → If you don't have testimonials, insert a from ____ to ____ statement.

How do you get testimonials that sell? Use the following examples to get testimonials that sell.

Option 1

In your final call, ask questions and celebrate the success of your client. Ask the following questions:

- What are some of the biggest changes you've noticed since working together?
- What was one of your favorite parts of this experience?

Celebrate their success. Brag on them. Write down what they say. Ask if you can use it in testimonials in a follow-up email.

Option 2 → Testimonial Request Take-n-Tweak Email (Small Offer)

[Insert Greeting],

I hope you are doing well and continuing to benefit from our sessions.

You were so kind as to share your feedback about how Authentic Selling influenced your business. I wanted to thank you for sharing your experience with me. It's so moving to hear how my work can impact amazing people like you. You have no idea how much it meant to me.

Would you consider taking a moment to write a brief testimonial about your experience working with me? It really helps others who are considering making the same investment understand what to expect from the material I share.

Also if there is anything I can do for you moving forward, please reach out and let me know.

Insert closing

Option 3 → Testimonial Request Take-n-Tweak Email (Small Offer)

[Insert Greeting],

I have enjoyed working with you these past [insert time frame]. It was so exciting to see [insert something specific]. To help me find more clients just like you, would you mind answering a few questions about your experience with me?

I value your feedback and strive to create raving fans. I read every single line of feedback, take it to heart, and make every attempt to improve upon my process from your answers.

Thank you in advance for your time.

1. On a scale of 1–10 (1 being, "Not at all" and 10 being, "Hell yes, absolutely love it!") how satisfied are you with this experience?
2. What are some of the biggest changes you've noticed since working together?
3. Are you getting what you need to move forward? (If no, what do you need or desire more of?)
4. What was one of your favorite parts of this experience?
5. What is something you'd like me to change?
6. Is there anything else you'd like me to know?

Option 4 → Testimonial Request Take-n-Tweak Email (Course/Class)

Sales School Testimonials

- What was the best thing about Sales School?
- What did you learn in Sales School that allowed you to make more money in your business?
- Why should a business owner make the investment in Sales School?
- How much money have you made in your business using the Authentic Selling strategies taught in Sales School?
- Is there anything unique about Kendrick's style of teaching?
- Is there anything you want to share?

Option 5 → Testimonial Request Take-n-Tweak Email (Combining All the Methods)

[Insert greeting],

I am checking to see how you are doing since our work together. I genuinely enjoyed getting to know you and helping you achieve [insert desired outcome or a pain point you helped them work through].

Your Authentically Written Sales Page Copy

I would also love some input from you. Would you be willing to share a few sentences about your experience working with me? It really helps me help others facing similar issues, as I am continually working to improve the outcomes for my clients.

Thank you for taking the time to share. I value your time. Please let me know if I can further support you in any way.

[Insert closing]

(Optional) Frequently Asked Questions (FAQs)

If you add an FAQ section, do it in an "accordion-style" like the example later in the chapter.

Authentic Selling® Sales Page Formula

- Step 1: Attention
- Step 2: Interest
- Step 3: Transition to What's Possible
- Step 4: Desire
- Step 5: Transition to Trust
- Step 6: Features + Benefits
- Step 7: Why You Statement
- Step 8: Investment/Call to Action
- Step 9: Buy Me Now Statement
- Step 10: Results/Testimonials

Let's take a look at the full page, shall we darling? And then in the next chapter we'll jump into how to get into your buyer's brain.

Example Sales Page

Attention

You have the life-changing idea, the die-hard commitment, and all the deliverables to make a real difference in the world … but if you don't know how to articulate that value to interested buyers your business is broke. Or worse – a very expensive hobby.

Interest

- Hustling harder and harder, month after month, and STILL not cracking $50K in revenue?
- Sinking more and more money into your business and not seeing ANY returns?
- Wasting valuable time on free consult calls that always seem to end with potential clients going missing in action (MIA) (or courting your competitors; ugh)?
- Telling yourself – "I just CAN'T do sales!" ...
- Sitting on a sales call palms sweating, trying desperately not to sound, well ... desperate?
- Wondering if potential customers can tell you're new at this?
- Pricing your offers wrong and thinking it's probably not even worth that much?
- Throwing in some extras is the only way you can seal the deal?
- End your day feeling like more of a fraud than an expert?

You're ready to give up. You just don't have what it takes to do this. You're missing that killer, eye-of-the-tiger, take 'em down at all costs, predatory drive that you need to make the sale.

Transition to What's Possible

Imagine how it will feel when you close your first sale, your first $10K month, $50K month, or even your first million dollars.

Desire

- Learn how to sell with calm, unshakeable confidence (no more sweaty palms or self-doubt spirals).

- Effortlessly build loyal, long-lasting customer relationships (i.e. RAVING fans) – so you never have to worry about losing out to the competition.

- Handle objections with class and charm like a well-seasoned pro, and hear "YES!" on the regular.

- Consistently close sales in a way that feels like you're helping a friend – not harassing a stranger.

- End your sales calls with your customer BEGGING to work with you and handing over their credit card number! (They'll even thank YOU for the opportunity!)

- Be EXCITED to get on the phone with prospects, because you know how to have easy, engaging, and feel-good conversations that convert into clients – and big bucks.

- Have the confidence to create compelling, premium offers that you KNOW are worth every penny – so you can work smarter, not harder, and finally make the money you need to have the freedom you want.

- Generate major buzz on social media about your services and products that lead to month-long wait lists, sold-out masterminds, and five-figure launches.

Transition to Trust

You can do ALL that while still being your authentic, helpful, genuine, brilliant, charming self. You CAN find your customers, share your products and services, AND create raving fans like the real, connected, heart-centered person and change-maker that you actually are. The whole "won't take no for an answer" way of making sales is old and outdated. More importantly, people are tired of it.

Features + Benefits

Welcome to Sales School, the #1 sales training for your business.

Sales School is a seven-week interactive program backed by high-touch expert coaching, results-driven training, and long-term support like nothing else out there.

The step-by-step process we teach will help you feel amazingly confident selling your products and services. You will learn the proven sales tools, systems, and strategies you've been missing, so you can attract loyal customers through genuine engagement and overcome objections with grace.

So that you can actually DO the work you're meant to do (AND make a living doing it).

Your business will make more money without you needing to be a sales bully.

- Sales School will provide you the tools to go from struggling to find your customers to actually doing the work you're meant to do (AND make a living doing it).
- You'll go from feeling like you've tried everything when it comes to marketing but nothing's working to making more money without you needing to be a sales bully.
- Built a big, beautiful business model but still can't manage to build a big, beautiful bank account? Learn to convert 50% more potential customers by mastering your follow ups and turning a "maybe" into "where do I sign!"

Whether you're trying to land your first paying client or trying to hit the 100K mark, Sales School provides you with proven sales tools, systems, and strategies you've been missing, so you can attract loyal customers through genuine engagement and overcome objections with grace.

Why You Statement

Sales School was created for people just like you – honest business owners who want an ick-free, easily repeatable, step-by-step process for selling so you can make more money and a bigger difference without selling your soul.

You may not be able to see it right now but I can! I've lived it! I've taught more than 1,000 other students in 186 countries who have lived it, and I want you to live it, too!

You deserve a business that makes you money.

So if what you've been doing isn't working . . . (and you've got the bank statements to prove it) . . .

You've got a sales problem. The good news is – learning to sell isn't rocket science!

Features + Benefits

Welcome to Sales School, the #1 sales training for your business

Sales School is a seven-week interactive program backed by high-touch expert coaching, results-driven training, and long-term support like nothing else out there.

The step-by-step process we teach will help you feel amazingly confident selling your products and services. You will learn the proven sales tools, systems, and strategies you've been missing, so you can attract loyal customers through genuine engagement and overcome objections with grace.

So that you can actually DO the work you're meant to do (AND make a living doing it).

Your business will make more money without you needing to be a sales bully.

- Sales School will provide you the tools to go from struggling to find your customers to actually doing the work you're meant to do (AND make a living doing it).

- You'll go from feeling like you've tried everything when it comes to marketing but nothing's working to making more money without you needing to be a sales bully.

- Built a big, beautiful business model but still can't manage to build a big, beautiful bank account? Learn to convert 50% more potential customers by mastering your follow-ups and turning a "maybe" into "where do I sign!"

Whether you're trying to land your first paying client or trying to hit the 100K mark, Sales School provides you with proven sales tools, systems, and strategies you've been missing, so you can attract loyal customers through genuine engagement and overcome objections with grace.

Today, I'm one of the top sales coaches in the business – and I'm KNOWN for getting results.

Investment/Call to Action

Choose the Authentic Selling® University Plan That Works Best for You

One Payment of	Four Monthly Payments of	Ten Monthly Payments of
$4,000	$1,000	$400
USD	US	USD
Join now	Join now	Join now

DUE TO THE EXCEPTIONAL LEVEL OF ATTENTION THAT YOU RECEIVE DURING SALES SCHOOL, CLASS SIZE IS LIMITED TO ONLY 100 STUDENTS PER SEMESTER.

Buy Me Now Statement

Ready to shortcut years of trying to figure out sales skills on your own by trial and error? Learn proven strategies to make sales with empathy and get real support from a sales expert every step of the way. Sales School is waiting for you.

Each semester is limited to 100 students only to make sure you get the attention you deserve.

Results/Testimonials

Don't take my word for it. Take a look at what our amazing alumni have to say you can expect in Sales School.

"You've gone above and beyond in giving and over-giving to help us. Your genuine concern for our ability to learn and incorporate our learning into our business warms my heart. Your program is a role model to me of how to over-deliver value!" – Jo Ann Kobuke

"I was able to create a consistent and effective message in every medium that I use to communicate . . . the website copy, sales call, and social media. This course is fabulous." – Carla Hightower

"Before I entered Sales School, I had a big business dream and an even bigger fear of talking about my work. Whenever anyone mentioned the word 'sales' I simply stopped listening. Selling was scary and gross. Now, thanks to the care, compassion, and kick-ass content Kendrick and her team delivered, fear has morphed into courage, and confusion has become clarity. I enthusiastically embrace selling, because just like Kendrick promised it would, selling has become helping. And I love helping! Sales School works. Since graduating just a few weeks ago, four new authors have said yes. My business dream is becoming my business reality." – Michelle Radomski

"Investing in Sales School and Kendrick Shope was the BEST investment I've ever made. Hands down. I made my investment back two weeks before the training ended! I've never had that happen before. Sales School is THE most high-touch online program you'll ever find. I don't know how Kendrick does it all and still manages to laugh and look so fabulous! She has such a generous heart and is even more invested in your success than you are. Every question is answered. Every problem is solved. And what's incredible is the support I'm receiving as an alum!!! UH-MAZING!!! I just feel better waking up in the morning, knowing that Kendrick is part of my world. Business building is definitely less lonely with Kendrick by my side." – Uma Girish

FAQs

Still have questions? We've got answers!

QUESTION & ANSWER

You talk about results a lot. How can I be sure I'll get the ones I want?
- This isn't your typical sink-or-swim online course. As soon as Sales School starts, you're going to have a place to start with your win/win document. You'll share with me the three goals you want to accomplish with your investment, and I'm going to help you get there, checking in with you along the way.

Sales School seems steep. $4,000 is a big chunk of change, no?

- But selling is a skill set that makes your business money FOR LIFE (and totally worth the less than $5.50 you'll be spending a day on Sales

School if you ask me). Without the ability to sell, your business can't survive. The good news is: Most of my students recoup their investment in a matter of months (some have even made their money back in a day by using ONE of the follow-up scripts in the bonus library).

- Plus, you'll get your 90-day no fail plan when you join Sales School, which outlines every step you need to begin making your investment back.
- I've thoughtfully tailored Sales School to make it practically impossible for you to fail, as long as you do your part.

I've got a copywriter. Do I really need Sales School, too?

- Copywriters can help you sound like a pro, but they aren't there to help you handle yourself like one when you're talking to potential clients on the fly, via email, or on an initial call. Sales School teaches you the art of Authentic Selling®, so you can know exactly what to say and how to say it in a way that feels true to you without any slime or grime.

I've taken other courses and gotten zero results. What makes Sales School any different?

- I'm thrilled you asked. Unlike most group training programs, the level of hands-on support and commitment you'll be getting from me in Sales School is pretty much unprecedented and makes getting real results easier than ever.
- I'll be blunt: You need to implement what you learn, and you'll only get out of Sales School what you put in (like most things in life). What I can promise you is NO student is left behind.

Do I need to have my niche figured out before enrolling in Sales School?

- In short, yes. Sales School will help you learn how to speak in a way that converts. But you'll need to understand your niche to be able to communicate with your ideal clients.

Is Sales School for product-based businesses or service-based businesses?

- Both! No matter what kind of business you run, Sales School teaches you sales principles that'll help attract and woo customers and keep them committed.

- While our syllabus does cover some topics specific to service-based businesses (like consult calls, email scripts for follow-ups, etc.), you'll also learn how to write high-converting sales copy, all about social selling, and how to talk about what you're selling in a way that's engaging and genuine – which is perfect for in-person networking and marketing situations!

Is Sales School only for coaches?

- Definitely not! Some of the most successful Sales School graduates have been B2C and B2B business owners. You'll find everyone from graphic designers, to coaches, to photographers, to nutritionists, to psychics, to estheticians and product makers in here.

I'm so busy with my business, what if I don't have time to complete the training and homework?

- You get lifetime access to both the video training library and study hall Facebook Community. Plus, all of our live coaching calls are recorded. So while you'll get more value out of following along with us, participating in weekly tutor times, and having your homework reviewed by me, Sales School is designed to be easily accessible and fit into your schedule when it's most convenient for you.

Is there a payment plan?

- Yes, you asked and I listened! You can choose to pay $4,000 up front
- You have the option to either make 4 monthly installments of $1,000 Or 10 installments of $400.

For each plan, the first payment will be due upon signing up.

Chapter 9

Your Buyer's Brain

Authentic Selling® Quote: "If they don't know you, they will not buy from you."

– Kendrick Shope

Authentic Selling® Gems from Chapter 9

◆ Find people who are excited to purchase from you.

◆ Understand a record scratch moment.

◆ Why most opt-ins fail.

Authentic Selling® Definition: the words *hook, record scratch moment, attention-getting statement,* and *headline* when used in this chapter all mean the same thing and will be used interchangeably.

In Chapter 1 we talked about, if you feel icky, sleazy, slimy or gross about selling through cold calling, email, or social media, you're not alone. Most of us have gotten dumb, unsolicited, annoying pitches from people we don't know.

Blindly contacting people sucks and doesn't work.

So take a breath because I'm not going to ask you to do that. Such pitches are outside of the Sales Guardrail for most people because they are icky, sleazy, slimy, and gross. I'm gonna share another secret with you right now, which just so happens to be the reason why this tactic feels so inappropriate and icky to most of us. It's because this technique is kinda CRAZY.

Think about it.

This person doesn't know you at all. There's no past relationship. This would be like someone sitting next to you on a plane asking you to give them money as soon as you sit down. You wouldn't do that unless you had all the free drinks in the lounge beforehand, and probably not even then. In business speak we call this a zippity-doo-dah way of getting right to the sale; a lack of engagement.

Here's another example from the real world. When I was working in pharma sales, we used to go to networking events. A lot of industries have these – for younger people, for new folks, and even for seasoned veterans. The whole point of a networking event is to create and build relationships, whether that's between vendors and clients, teams and leaders, or colleagues at different companies. It's usually pretty casual. You chat in a small group, see a benefit in having a relationship with someone and then exchange business cards. But there's always that one person running around handing their business cards to everyone.

This chapter is not about that either. Instead, I will teach you all the ways to engage your audience and potential customers in conversation. And those conversations? Aren't all selling.

Clarissa had a problem, y'all. She had created a company, She Rocks @ College, to help students like herself succeed. In fact, she wasn't making the money she expected and that meant she was not helping the people she was passionate about helping, the next generation of women who were smart but needed support to get top grades. She Rocks @ College wasn't exactly rocking but this was about more than a business that makes money; this was personal for Clarissa, and my hunch is your business is much the same.

Let's rewind. By the time Clarissa was in her own junior year, she had already failed out of seven courses and had an advisor tell her that she wasn't smart enough to succeed in medicine. (Talk about icky, sleazy, slimy, and gross! Who says that?)

Like you, Clarissa believed in herself and her dreams. She wasn't going to let her past grades and some jerk insulting her stand in the way of her goal of being a nurse. She went home and did a ton of research. Over time, Clarissa figured out how to study effectively and help herself deal with the feelings of overwhelm, anxiety, and insecurity that undermined her super smart self.

And once she became a successful RN, she wanted to pay it forward and bam! She Rocks @ College was born. Clarissa was passionate about helping the next generation of women who were smart but needed support to get top grades.

When Clarissa found out about Authentic Selling®, she had only generated $11,000 in revenue that entire year. One of the reasons she signed up for my buyer psychology training was because she felt out of sync with her customers. Only 30% of her sales calls turned into a sale, because most of the students she talked to said that they were too broke to pay for her help. However, after Clarissa learned what I'm going to teach you in this chapter – and just this chapter – she made $11,000 in a month and closed 83% of her calls.

You might be thinking, Kendrick, how is that possible? Well, you're going to learn how to do business differently. Trust the redhead, each of your prospects is different. What motivates them to buy is different, too. Understanding what motivates your customer to purchase is one of the most important aspects of running a successful business. That's why I'm dedicating an entire chapter to it, because understanding why, how, and when your clients buy can make the difference between an $11,000 year and $11,000 month – just like it did for Clarissa.

Why It Matters

This is most likely self-explanatory but never assume your reader or potential client understands what you think is self-explanatory. A great example of this is when I first quit my top-performing corporate job and began taking classes to learn how to run a business. I was reading this fantastic sales page online and the letters *D-I-Y* are all over the page. I know this will seem unbelievable but I did not know what DIY (Do It Yourself) meant. I guess that says a lot about my love of doing things myself! Despite having a deep connection to the sales page, I did not purchase this particular class because the creator assumed I knew what DIY meant. I read that page 10 times y'all, and I did not know so they lost a sale. My point is, do not assume your potential client understands something you believe is so easy to comprehend that you fail to explain it.

Back to Clarissa and why learning about different types of buyers matters to your business. You will close more sales, make more money, and help more people when you are aware of the Five Types of Buyers.

Your Buyer's Brain

In Authentic Selling®, we separate buyers into five categories: white, yellow, blue, green, and red.

These categories are based on science, but what I want you to recognize right off the bat is that we can change what psychology we are showing up with based on the day. Sometimes I wake up feeling like Beyoncé – energized and confident and with a gigantic smile on my face. But on other days, I feel the exact opposite – cranky, annoyed, ready to go back to bed before I'm even finished with my first cup of coffee. And guess what – your customers feel the same way, too!

Every customer is different, and what motivates them to buy can vary from customer to customer. Understanding what motivates your buyer to purchase is overlooked when it comes to running a modern business. You are taught to spend hours mapping out information about your ideal clients, but we never spend time thinking about what makes them actually click to purchase.

The easiest way to remember the colors are yellow and blue make green, and red and white make candy canes. Those are our sales psychology colors for our buyers: yellow, blue, green, red, and white.

Yellow: The Sunny Social Butterfly

Someone who is making a buying decision from a sun shiny yellow place is sociable, dynamic, enthusiastic, and persuasive on a good day. On a bad day, they could be excitable or frantic. Think of yellow as your sunny social butterfly. You have heard people say that stories sell, and they do, but they're not the only thing that sells. When you are using a story to sell, you are speaking to people who are in this yellow social butterfly frame of mind.

Blue: The Cautious and Precise Introvert

Unlike yellow, a blue person also has good day and bad day qualities. On a good day, someone who is in a blue sales psychology frame of mind is cautious, precise, questioning, and maybe a little formal. On a bad day, they could be stuffy, indecisive, suspicious, cold, or reserved. People making decisions who are in a blue frame of mind tend to be introverts. Unlike our yellows who are extroverts, they don't care about the story; they want the data – just the facts. This is where statistics and perhaps testimonials can be a great way of communication to help you sell.

Green: The Values-Based Buyer

There is a tendency to think all your people are green, but they're not. All your people have all these colors. What does it mean to be green? On a good day, you're caring, encouraging, sharing, or patient. On a bad day, you could be bland, docile, reliant on someone else, stubborn, or unwilling to go the extra mile. People who make decisions based on green sales psychology are making decisions off of their values. They are perhaps looking at the benefit beyond money or the benefit beyond what it means to them, and instead what it means to the whole world or what it means to their child.

Red: The Competitive Expert

When people are in a red frame of mind, they don't want your story, your green values, your blue statistics or testimonials, or your data. They already view themselves as the expert. On a good day, people who are making decisions from a red sales psychology point of view are competitive, determined, strong-willed, and purposeful. On a bad day, they're aggressive, controlling, overbearing, and intolerant.

When you are using red sales psychology to sell, your posts are usually based on something super quick. It could be fear of missing out, last chance, or the idea that all the other experts are doing it. They're going to get lost in the story and think they don't have time to read it, or they're going to get weighed down by the data. The values are not important to them right now in this moment, so we've got to get their attention quickly.

White: The Ready-to-Buy Fan

You'll notice there aren't any examples for white because white doesn't need examples. Someone who is white is already sold. They may have heard some of your yellow stories, been moved by some of your blue data, further committed to buy from you and only you because of some of your green values, and realized that now is the time because of some of your red buyer's brain selling.

White is ready to buy. These people are either raving fans, repeat customers, or people who, the minute you say they can buy, say, "Show me where." They don't need all this other stuff. White gets left out a lot, but these are the people who are early adopters. They're ready to go. We don't need to bog them down with all this other stuff; we just need to give them a place to pay.

Using the Buyer Psychology Colors in Your Sales Process Now you understand that all buyers' brains are not the same all the time. You understand that we are a mess of contradictions and that one day I may be extremely motivated to buy from you because you shared your values, because you shared your love of New Kids On the Block. The reason my first $5,000 customer bought from me was because I unabashedly shared my love for New Kids On the Block. That would be a value, a green type of buyer's brain reason that she decided to work with me. Of course, that's not the only reason; there had to be some blue in there to prove to her that I knew what I was talking about, and probably some red and some yellow also.

You understand that one type of sales presentation probably isn't going to work all the time. We need to be able to at least hit the yellow, blue, green, red, and even white. If you're a pharmaceutical sales rep and you're thinking, "I get 60 seconds; there is no way I can do yellow, blue, green, red," I understand. You're right. But that's not the goal for each of your interactions. The goal of your interaction is to move the conversation forward.

Finding People Happy to Buy from You

Prospecting is basically how you're going to find customers. This is a full chapter about prospecting but you're probably not going to need to do all of these prospecting activities. Nevertheless, readers and students tell me they come back to this section over and over because without prospecting, your business has no customers.

Have you ever had thoughts like:

- Where are my customers?
- How do I stand out?
- Where are my people?

If your potential customers don't know you, it is impossible for them to become your customer. Too many people discount this step. It's tried, true, and tested in arguably the most high-stakes industry that exists, the American political arena. I'm a bit of a nerd when it comes to reading books, and one of my favorite topics is presidential memoirs. Would you believe when a candidate does one thing and does it well, 100% of the time it worked and they won their election? It spans multiple decades and much like selling it can be done icky, sleazy, slimy, or with a hint of authenticity. I'm not naive enough to believe that the good of the country is all these people had in mind but it's worth noticing when successful people do something consistently. What is this thing that is so powerful that you can also use in your business? It goes back to the Kendrickism "If your prospects don't know you, it's impossible for them to buy from you."

Future presidents chose to invest time going from diner to diner, hosting teas, and small events to present the candidate not only as an experienced politician but also as a family man with strong values. During these smaller events potential voters who may have felt discounted by Washington in the past have a chance to discuss policies and platforms that matter to voters in small towns. These smaller events were in personal settings making potential voters feel involved and valued. It's no different than how you've been learning to make connections that matter with your prospects.

What Does This Have to Do with You?

Candidates for one of the most powerful positions in the world, US presidents, take the time to prospect in a way that creates connection and makes prospects feel valued. Did you ever think of running for president as a sales job, and when they need new voters, they rely on an Authentic Selling® Foundation because it works? This falls back to what you learned in Chapter 3: All things being equal friends buy from friends. All things being unequal friends buy from friends. If it works for the politicians who are often now well thought of, this will work for you and your business.

Authentic Selling® Prospecting Method #1

Authentic Selling® Opt-In

Every industry that has an online presence has a prospecting process and most start with an opt-in.

What is an opt-in?

An Authentic Selling® opt-in is an exchange of information where the potential customer gives you an email address and your business provides some type of information to your potential customer free of charge. An opt-in is a way for your business to get an email address and add a potential customer or prospect to your email list so that you can prospect to them. That's it. Pure, plain, and simple.

You may have heard opt-ins called a pink spoon or a freebie. The term *pink spoon* comes from Baskin Robbins, where you get a sample of ice cream with a pink spoon. If you have a craving for mocha chip, a little sample won't fulfill that craving – you'll want the entire ice cream. That's what an opt-in is, a sample. Think about the questions your people are asking, where they're getting stuck, and their desired outcome.

The "free things" could be all sorts of items. It could be on your website, it could be a free training, it could be to get first access. Whatever it is, there is an exchange here. Your prospect is giving you their email address, you are giving them something free. Spoiler alert! We're not there yet, but spoiler alert.

Authentic Selling® Pro Tip → People rarely, and by rarely, I almost want to say never, opt-in for updates, for newsletters. Do you want a newsletter?

Do you want another email clogging your inbox because you're getting an update? No, probably not. So, if your opt-in or your copy on your website says opt-in for updates or opt-in for inspiration or opt-in for motivation, I'm going to challenge you on that and say, why? Why? What is this gonna do for me, your potential buyer?

Authentic Selling® Pro Tip → You have got to make sure that your opt-in sells. Do you need one? 100% yes. Period. If you run an online business, you need one.

A big problem businesses have is they slap up an opt-in and then it doesn't convert because sales language is never considered. Language must grab your prospect's attention. Remember, your customer is usually multi-tasking. You need to plan for your customers to be scrolling and dealing with other things when your prospects are first exposed to your opt-in.

Your opt-in will be one of the first things that people who are new to you will consume. Think of your opt-in as an appetizer or taster of your product or services. It needs to be incredibly compelling to grab people's attention. The mistake businesses make is learning they need an opt-in and as overachievers, like you and me, they take action but don't consider the language they use and how it will grab a prospect. Using your Authentic Selling® Sales Map will disrupt the scroll when you use pain points and benefits of your product or services as your attention-getting copy, your hook, your headline. An opt-in does a business no good if it's just an opt-in. Your opt-in must lead to selling. Throughout the book, we've discussed that most parts of your business need to be run through the lens of selling and by failing to do that, it will not convert prospects into buyers.

Types of Opt-Ins

Soft opt-in is one where your prospect simply has to check a box and agree to receive emails within the terms and conditions of a website.

An example is by checking here you agree to the terms and conditions. Within the terms and conditions you will have language about permission to email.

Hard opt-in is one where your prospect directly consents to providing their email address in exchange for something you will provide them. This type of opt-in can be discounts, free trials, pdf, webinar.

Retailers like Nordstrom and Pottery Barn use opt-ins by having you enter your email so they can sell you via email at a later date and in return you will receive 15% off. Vanguard uses the promise of a true partner in investing by providing you with a guide to help you get started.

Sample opt-in used at kendrickshope.com.

DISCOVER #1 SALES TREND

THAT'S GONNA ROCK THE ONLINE MARKET FOR YEARS TO COME.

Disrupt the Scroll. Stand Out. Make Sales.

Name*

Email*

Text opt-ins/QR codes are the most popular currently. We see them used on TV ads, and I use them when speaking. The use of QR opt-ins is increasing because of the ease of opting in from a smartphone and TV/computer by simply clicking a QR code.

An example I use is "Text sales" to insert number to receive proven opt-ins that convert.

If you have an opt-in and it's not creating potential customers for your business, remember that people are busy. We've talked about this in Chapter 8: we've got to disrupt the scroll, get attention, and we've got to make it KISS.

KISS: Keep It Super Simple when prospecting customers. If your opt-in isn't converting, start by disrupting the scroll. Your language has got to be so compelling that they're like, oh my God, I know why I want this, give it to me now.

Five Steps to Creating Your Authentic Selling® Opt-In

Step 1: What's the Modality Going to Be?

- PDF
- Meditation

- Guides
- Sample chapters
- Video training
- Discount
- Checklist → generally has one of the highest conversions

Step 2: What's the Content of the Opt-In Going to Be?

What solution are your prospects searching for at night while scrolling their phones? What pain point can you create a freebie about? You can also think back to Chapter 8 when you learned to write your sales page. What was the first step of that process? Just as you did in Chapter 8 and writing your sales page, the first step is to grab your prospects' attention. That's what your opt-in content needs to do, too.

Attention → You have to grab the attention and in today's competitive world, you must have something that creates a record scratch moment for your customer.

You know the moment when a record is stopped suddenly, with the sound of the needle sliding across the record? This moment is a record scratch moment, which has become a popular culture sound to indicate a sudden or abrupt interruption. It creates a dramatic pause that indicates a moment is so dramatic it causes people to pause and pay attention.

- What questions are my potential customers asking?
- What are they Googling? Where do they have problems?
- What is their desired outcome? Think about their desired outcome and where they might get stuck.

Authentic Selling® Pro Tip → Your opt-in is a micro solution to a problem or the first step in solving a problem. It does NOT solve the entire problem. Simplifying your content is almost always a good idea. Instead of long, comprehensive content, break it down.

Example: If you're writing about emails that convert, focus on three common mistakes rather than every single step to creating emails that convert.

Deep vs. Wide Content

You have to make a choice with your content, specifically your opt-in content, and decide if you want to go deep or wide as you teach this content.

Deep content is extremely detailed. Deep content provides detailed, comprehensive information on a single topic, like Authentic Selling®. Let's continue with the earlier example of "Writing Emails That Convert." You've drilled down to talking about three common mistakes. If you were going to teach those tools using a Deep framework you would teach all three of those common mistakes.

Deep Content Example: Three Common Mistakes Creating Emails That Convert

1. You could list the three mistakes:
   - Mistake 1 Weak subject line
   - Mistake 2 Poor call to action
   - Mistake 3 Overly self-focused content
2. Describe or support why those three things are considered mistakes.
3. Show examples and explain how to correct those three mistakes.
4. Share why the above works.
5. Advise where the reader might get hung up or stuck.
6. Tell the reader how to self-check to make sure they get the desired results.

When you use the Deep framework, you need to make sure that you are able to show your potential customer there is still more to learn so that they understand and can see the need to purchase from you.

Wide content is broad, providing awareness that certain tools exist but only go in-depth on a few aspects. Using the same example, Authentic Selling® Tools Writing Emails That Convert, you drilled down to talking about three common mistakes. If you were to teach those mistakes through a Wide framework, you would make the person consuming the material aware of all three mistakes but only teach one of three in depth by providing all the steps. The other two mistakes you would simply list and create awareness about those mistakes.

Wide Content Example: Three Common Mistakes Creating Emails That Convert

1. First you could list the three mistakes:
   - Mistake 1 Weak subject line
   - Mistake 2 Poor call to action
   - Mistake 3 Overly self-focused content
2. Describe or support why one of those three things is considered a mistake.
3. Show examples and explain how to correct the same one of the three.

    Share why one of the three above works.
4. Advise where the reader might get hung up or stuck on using the same one of the three.
5. Tell the reader how to self-check using the same one of the three to make sure they get the desired results.

You will not solve the entire problem with any opt-in. Instead, you are creating awareness about this pain point you can solve. Awareness is a good opt-in. You're aware of three things keeping your business stuck or broke, and then you decide you want to consume more from this person who created this incredible opt-in!

Authentic Selling® Pro Tip → One of the easiest ways to find what type of content you want to create is to observe how industry leaders break down topics and present their content and apply similar strategies with your unique spin. Notice I did not say copy or steal ideas but there is nothing wrong with being inspired by someone's content.

Avoid Common Content Mistakes

1. Overcomplication: Keep It Super Simple (KISS) and to the point.
2. Long Personal Stories: Ensure the reader sees themselves in the content.
3. Incomplete Problem Solving: Focus on solving a subset of their problem.

Step 3: What's the Title of Your Opt-In Going to Be?

The title is the most important part of your opt-in because it is what creates the attention, the record scratch moment. At Authentic Selling® we've tested headlines and these are the top five attention-getting statements that convert the best.

Number Titles

Titles that begin with numbers and "how to" headlines perform as the highest converting headlines according to our tests. What's important for you to know is that numbers and how-to headlines also perform at the top of the list when most companies test headlines to get data on what performs. One important note is not to use a number that seems overwhelming like 125 or 5,000.

- Three Ways to Eat Pizza Daily and Lose Weight
- Six Problems All Married Women Understand
- Seven Shocking Statistics That Will Change Your Business
- Four Must Have Jeans for Fall
- Five Ways You're Aging Yourself
- Ten of the Best TV Shows of All Time

How-to Titles

"How-to" and Number headlines are the top of the top performers but "How-to" is the easiest attention-getting statement to create in my opinion. You start with the words "How to" _____ and you fill in the blank copy from your Sales Map using either pain points or benefits. Told y'all we were going to use your Authentic Selling® Sales Map and it would save you time to knock it out.

- How to Avoid Getting Knocked Out by Your Dog
- How to Eat Pizza Daily and Lose Weight
- How to Look Younger When You Feel over the Hill
- How to Overcome Objections with Confidence
- How to Decorate Small Spaces

Reader Responsibility Titles

Reader Responsibility headlines are meant to provide a record scratch moment, grabbing attention of your prospect, and creating a sense of urgency. Your potential customers should feel a bit of "I must read this" or "listen to this." You've experienced this before, when you see a piece of content and think "ohh, before I do whatever the headline references, I need to read, watch, listen to, this piece of content."

- The Sunscreen Every Mom Needs to Avoid
- The Diet Craze You Must Check Out
- The Insider's Tip to Art Shopping
- The Secret Beauty Pill Hollywood Doesn't Want You to Know About
- The Key to Headlines That Convert You May Be Missing
- The Pro Advice You Need to Hit a Million in Business
- The Secret to a Happy Marriage You Need to Know

Informational Titles

Informational titles are meant to provide clarity and relevance. These headlines are the most direct and are known for brevity. Get straight to the point and be done. Once again your Sales Map can be referred to here to create powerful copy.

- Ways to Make Work More Fun
- Advice on Happy Marriages
- Statistics That Will Improve Selling
- Tips to Cook Healthy Meals Your Family Will Love
- Understanding Depression
- Surviving Bed Rest
- Best Websites for Shopping

Question Titles

One of my favorite headlines are questions. Think about the questions your customer is googling, what solutions they would pay you to know. What do you believe is the one question your prospects think the answer to would solve all their problems? A great question to ask yourself is would this "question title" get your attention if you saw it on social media?

- What Are Creative Ways to Get More Customers?
- When Is IT Going to Happen?
- Who Is the Next President?
- Life Balance. Is It Possible?
- Want to Make Money and Help Others?
- What's for Dinner?
- Is Singing a Talent That Can Be Learned?

Step 4: What Is the Call to Action of Your Opt-In?

Make sure that your opt-in has a call to action to continue the conversation. A call to action is a statement you use at the end of your opt-in to get the viewer to move onto the next step. But remember what we said about calls to action. Don't have 5,000. Have one. Instead of just saying "leave a comment," ask a specific, open-ended question to encourage engagement:

Example Call to Action That Can Be Used When Posting Opt-In on Social Media: "What is one area you'll take action on in your sales today as a result of this lesson? Share below, and I'll reply!"

Example Call to Action to Entice Readers to Opt-In at the End of a Podcast, Blog, or YouTube Video. "Get started today and lose five pounds in five days. Click here. It's free!"

- Start your free trial today
- Try it free
- Get started
- Your next step to health begins here
- Your baby's sleep begins today
- Making money in your business starts here
- Learn more
- Learn how, here. It's free.
- Get started with your healthier lifestyle today
- A healthier lifestyle starts here
- Experience the difference
- Next Steps
  Enroll

  OR

  Have questions? Wonder if this is the right step for you? Email insert your email/contact info to get your questions answered.

- Next Steps

    Fill out the application here. You will be contacted within 24 hours to schedule a no-obligation sales chat. Taking control of your business sales has never been so fun.

    Let's get started.

- Next Steps

    Schedule your no-obligation consult here. Taking control of your business sales has never been so fun. Let's get started.

Choose the Authentic Selling® University Plan That Works Best for You

One Payment of	Four Monthly Payments of	Ten Monthly Payments of
$4,000	$1,000	$400
USD	USD	USD
Join now	Join now	Join now

- Ready to shortcut years of trying to figure out sales skills on your own by trial and error? Learn proven strategies to make sales with empathy and get real support from a sales expert every step of the way. Sales School is waiting for you.

Step 5: Create Trust

You create trust by concluding your opt-in with a short professional bio.

Authentic Selling® Pro Tip → Don't rely on other places to store your prospects for you. Facebook, Instagram, Pinterest, Twitter, YouTube – all are great places to prospect, at least from an online perspective. But you are subject to the rules of Facebook, Twitter, Instagram, Pinterest, YouTube, and they can change their rules at any time. So your goal is to move the conversation from social media to an email list you are in control of.

Think about it, what if social media says tomorrow you have to pay $1 million to have a business account? Oh, holy wow, then that's a problem. So you want to drive the conversation from the point of entry to a collective place where you hold email addresses. Usually that's called a CRM, Customer Relationship Management.

Post your opt-in on social media regularly, which brings us to the next type of prospecting you can use to attract new potential customers to your work.

Authentic Selling® Prospecting Method #2

Social Media

It does you no good to put an opt-in on your website or a podcast, blog, or vlog up, and fail to drive traffic (prospects) to it.

Each time that you post a blog, vlog, podcast you need to get the maximum return and the most number of eyes on it. You do this by creating social media to entice people to read or listen.

You should also be posting your opt-in at least one time a week on social media to stay relevant and expose your products and services to new potential customers.

In the old days, the way to prospect was

1. Knocking on doors
2. Cold calling
3. Telemarketing

I've done all three and none of those are super fun even for me, someone who loves selling. But then social media was invented and it opened doors that were once closed for modern businesses. Social media instantly expanded your potential to include the entire world, and you can reach them from the beach, your bedroom, or wherever you desire. Let me be crystal clear, social media is a great way to prospect and have customers find your business. But the goal is to move that conversation off social media to your email list or a sales call. Social media is key because:

- 3.2 billion people use social media.
- 78% of salespeople engaged in social selling are outselling their peers who aren't.

- 90% of top salespeople are already using social selling tools.
- Social sellers are 51% more likely to achieve sales quotas.
- Companies with consistent social selling processes are 40% more likely to hit revenue goals than non-social sellers.
- 84% of C-level executives use social media to make purchasing choices.

One Post Created 48 New Leads

When my student Vanessa joined Authentic Selling®, she was hesitant to sell on Instagram because of concerns about being pushy with her audience of aspiring artists. After we talked about how to start and have authentic conversations on social media, I helped Vanessa craft a question about being a starving artist in her stories. We used the question headline tool from earlier in the chapter.

After Vanessa posed the question in her story, she used an Authentic Selling® Tool. She had 43 comments answering her questions within 24 hours, which was substantial since a lot of people follow her on Instagram just to see her artwork and tend not to read her captions. Once Vanessa had successfully prospected her ideal client, it was time to move on to the second step of selling and engage these folks in conversation. That's where you're going to see whether those people need your help, and it's not going to feel gross because you're just texting back and forth.

1. **Headline/Subject**: Grab attention.
2. **Lesson**: Provide valuable, actionable insights.
3. **Call to Action**: Encourage immediate engagement.

Avoiding Pitfalls

Crickets

Authentic Selling® Definition → Crickets: refers to when a piece of content gets little to no response from the audience. Crickets is a part of business growth in the beginning; after all, if prospects don't know you they are likely not going to take the time to comment on a social media post,

Consistency is key. Comments and engagement will come with time.

Inspiration or Consistency

Find ways to stay inspired and motivated to create content consistently, even when inspiration doesn't strike. Remember, your goal is to create valuable, engaging content that serves your audience's needs while guiding them to opt-in and take the next step with you. Consistency and strategic content planning are keys to success.

Authentic Selling® Prospecting Method #3

Authentic Selling® Email Signature

This one is an easy one. If you have an email address, there is no reason to avoid this Authentic Selling® Prospecting Method. You can prospect by your email signature, and no, you don't have to go pay for a fancy shmancy email signature.

Recently I had a student tell me one of her customers shared that they purchased right from her email signature. How? The link to her opt-in was right there. So, let's pretend that the name of your opt-in is to lose five pounds in the next five days and it's free.

Literally, you would have your name and then you would use the Authentic Selling® Headline Tool to create your hook.

Examples

Number

> Three Ways to Lose 5 Pounds in the Next 5 Days. It's Free.
> Followed by a link to your squeeze page.

How To

How to Lose 5 Pounds in the Next 5 Days. It's Free.
Followed by a link to your squeeze page.

Reader Responsibility

Must Do Before You Lose Another Pound. It's Free.
Followed by a link to your squeeze page.

Informational

Lose 5 Pounds in the Next 5 Days. It's Free.
Followed by a link to your squeeze page.

Now, don't get frustrated if you fail to get a customer from this. But, you just want to increase the likelihood that people actually opt-in for your free stuff. Add it to your email signature in your email provider, usually under settings, so you create it and don't think about it again.

There are more than 25 Prospecting Methods/How to Find Your Customers Methods taught in Authentic Selling®.

29 Places to Prospect

1. Email
2. Blog
3. Guest post
4. Newspaper ad
5. Feature
6. TV
7. Follow-up
8. Sales email
9. Advertise

10. Free talks
11. Tell three people a day what you do
12. Email signature
13. Connector
14. Webinar
15. Cold calling
16. Networking
17. Referral
18. Contest
19. Opt-In
20. Business card
21. Mini sessions
22. Private Facebook group
23. Pinterest
24. Keynote speaker
25. Podcast
26. Podcast guest
27. Newsletter
28. Author
29. Mini video series

Authentic Selling® Tools Takeaways

1. **Authentic Selling® Prospecting Methods**
   - Your Authentic Selling® Opt-In
   - Your Authentic Social Media
   - Your Authentic Selling® Email Signature
   - Your Authentic Selling® List of 29 Prospecting Methods

2. **Four Most Frequently Converted Headlines**
   - Number
   - How to
   - Informational
   - Reader Responsibility
3. **Authentic Selling® Calls to Action (CTAs)**
   - Authentic Selling® Done for You, CTAs Provided

Chapter 10

Your Authentic Business Plan

Authentic Selling® Quote: "You're entering your best business era yet."
– Kendrick Shope

Authentic Selling® Gems from Chapter 10

- ❖ Making money and helping others are not mutually exclusive.
- ❖ Putting it all together into Your Authentic Selling® Business Plan.

As we approach the end of this journey together, you've seen how selling can be more than just a transaction. You've uncovered the actual definition of selling and it has nothing to do with being pushy or as I like to say, icky, sleazy, slimy, gross, crusty, musty, rusty, or dusty! Your people need your offers. With Authentic Selling® you have a proven opportunity to build genuine connections, offer real value, and make a positive impact in the lives of others while getting paid well to do it. Making money and helping others are not mutually exclusive.

The First of Its Kind

Remember, Authentic Selling® is not about perfection; it's about being genuine and true to yourself. Your Authentic Selling® Sales Guardrail is always available to help you do a check-in with yourself to make sure you're honoring what is genuine to you as an individual. In fact, the ability to check in with your Authentic Selling® Sales Guardrail is one of the things that makes this process unique, like you. It's the first sales system of its kind that provides a tool for you to do a self-check so you can make certain you are within your integrity. It's able to be adapted to different people's comfort level so that you never have to do anything that feels off. A perfect example of what makes Authentic Selling® uniquely customizable is all of the different options provided to you to work through objections and close sales. Some of the options are less direct while others are super direct.

From the first tool you learned in the Authentic Selling® Orientation at the start of this book, your Fabulous Four, you learned that Authentic Selling® is rooted in understanding who you are, what you do, what is cool about you, why your prospect can trust you, and why that matters. Selling is turned into an act of helping and how you can help others through your unique products and services. By embracing Authentic Selling®, you can create meaningful relationships with your customers, avoid buyer's remorse, and create long-term success for your business.

Down the Rabbit Hole

In Chapter 2 we discussed the old way of selling versus the new authentic way of selling; but what I had to learn in my selling journey was the old way of running a successful business compared to the new way, a post-neurosurgery way of succeeding in business. I was on a path that was destined to lead to failure, trusting others more than I trusted myself. Isn't it ironic that I created this multi-million-dollar business that I believe makes a real difference alone, and when I got to a place of contentment, I started doubting my own decisions and second guessing every choice I made. I was afraid of failing but had zero awareness of that fear, which led me to end up failing. As my dad shared with us years ago, "Scared money won't make money," and that is where I found myself. Even if I had never had neurosurgery, I had been on a burn-it-all-down path in business.

A few years before neurosurgery, Halianna experienced a trauma that required our entire family to pitch in, lift her up, and help her to fall in love with life again. It was the most difficult time as a mom I've experienced to this point in my life. This happened toward the end of staying at home during the pandemic. We were all teetering on depression after being inside for months, wondering what was happening in our world. I felt it was up to me to get creative and find a way to make my entire family believe in life again.

But why stop there? I believed our Authentic Selling® community was suffering as well after dealing with a worldwide pandemic. I took on the responsibility of building up Halianna at one of the most crucial times in her life, pulling my family out of the funk from being stuck inside for months, and reinvigorating tens of thousands of people who were part of the community I created. I came up with the wildest, most far-fetched idea, but I've always had some pretty big dreams – many of which were out of the norm. An Olympic ice skater with no access to an ice skating rink is just one of those ideas I shared with you in this book.

The Idea

Picture it. One Night Only meets business masterclass right from the comfort of your own home, in your PJs or your nicest formal! One show, one night, one experience was created only for the Authentic Selling® community, their families, and no one else in the world. I wanted to bring the world's top talent to the Authentic Selling® community while we were stuck in our homes experiencing a global pandemic feeling scared, anxious, and frustrated. The community would have access to entertainment and learn from these entertainers who are at the top of their industry. One Night Only would be more than a night of music. The virtual curtain would go up on how to next-level your business.

Here's the concept: In an effort to inspire the Authentic Selling® community to maximize their own inner-potential, celebrated members of the Broadway community will share their insights and talents with Kendrick Shope's students, clients, and families while supporting the mission of Broadway Cares/Equity Fights AIDS (BCEFA). Through intimate interviews, curated conversations, and private performances, some of Broadway's biggest stars (both on and off the stage) will explore their own definition of success. This video event will marry the vibe of a TEDTalk or a masterclass with the thrill of a Broadway show. A specific focus on BELIEF and AUTHENTICITY will leave Kendrick Shope's clients/students feeling energized to bring the lessons from the creative arts into their own entrepreneurial ventures.

If you did not know it by now, I have massive dreams. What you read was the dream, how in the world was I going to make it happen? It would require me to close the biggest sale of my life.

The Biggest Sale of My Life

Important background information is that I did not know one person who works for BCEFA. This organization is one that receives six-figure donations from stars like Tom Hanks and Fortune 100 companies. Yet, I felt in my gut, my personal guardrail, I needed to at least make this ask of BCEFA for Halianna, my family, and my community. I teach tens of thousands of businesses each year that the word "No" is not rejection, just redirection and it would be out of integrity to let the fear of "No" stop me from taking a chance.

Step 1 of the Biggest Sale of My Life

I wondered if it was possible to host a first of its kind virtual Broadway show with some of the world's top stars. Not only did I have zero contacts at BCEFA, I had no idea how to even make something like this happen or what it would cost. I sent that email the only way I found to hopefully get in touch with someone at Broadway Cares. Well, the first step in securing a yes to my wild idea was getting someone to open this email that was from a complete stranger. Sound familiar? I had to succeed at Step 1 by creating an email headline or subject that stopped the scroll and got opened.

Step 2 of the Biggest Sale of My Life

Step 2 was creating the body of the email or copy that sells, meaning the email actually gets read. I did not have a reputation going for me in this space because no one was going to know me. I was a no name, tiny business, in Knoxville, Tennessee. I considered many of the Authentic Selling® Tools you've learned in this book starting with Keep It Super Simple (KISS).

I also started the email with a Genuine Thank You to BCEFA for the good work they put out into the world. Finally, I had to get my point across without having a super long email, so I wrote in short paragraphs followed by bullets, like you learned to do in Chapter 8. Finally remembering that prospects like to buy from experts, the body of my email had to be compelling enough to establish that I am someone who is serious about potentially raising money for BCEFA.

Step 3 of the Biggest Sale of My Life

Step 3 of this important sale was my call to action, which we've talked about in Chapters 8 and 9. We also learned that Authentic Selling® is not always about getting a yes or no, often it's about moving the conversation along to the next step. It's like your opt-in is intended to start the conversation providing a sample of your expertise. The CTA was an ask if we could hop on Zoom to discuss what seemed like an impossibly huge idea.

Step 4 of the Biggest Sale of My Life

BCEFA is the most loving, accepting organization I have ever had the pleasure of working with. They are top-rate humans and the day after I sent my email, I found that Steps 1–3 worked well enough to land a Zoom meeting with Director of Corp Giving Susan Slottoroff. Now I could not hide behind paragraphs and bullets, I had to show up and pitch to a woman who gets pitched by some of the biggest corporations in the world. I relied on a tool we have not talked about, which is usually reserved for what I call Upper Level Authentic Selling®. That doesn't mean that what we've covered together in the previous chapters won't work for more advanced sales; quite the opposite actually. You have to understand all that you dedicated yourself to learning in order to move onto Upper Level Authentic Selling®. Now that we are nearing the end of Authentic Selling®, you're ready to get a glimpse of Upper Level Authentic Selling®. The Upper Level Authentic Selling® Tool I used in my meeting with Susan is one I often used during my selling drugs era (still the legal kind y'all!). Authentic Selling® Vulnerability is a tool where you start a conversation by sharing something vulnerable. But not just anything, it needs to be relevant.

Authentic Selling® Warning you cannot fake this tool. You will crash and burn coming across as fake, icky, sleazy, slimy, gross, crusty, rusty, musty, or dusty.

Knowing this warning, there are a few times when Authentic Selling® Vulnerability is the exact tool you need, like my Step 4 in pitching Broadway Cares. I began this and many meetings with BCEFA by sharing this disclaimer. "I am very new, actually totally green, and have no idea what I am doing. But I follow directions well and you will not meet someone more passionate about making this a success for BCEFA. So please do not worry about my feelings, just shoot me straight with what's expected from me and if I missed something you need from me, tell me." Using the Authentic Selling® Vulnerability Tool made me feel less intimidated about being in a virtual room where I was underqualified. It takes courage to admit you're green but something surprising happens when you use this tool in the right context. You look like an expert even though you just said you don't know what you're doing!

Step 5 of the Biggest Sale of My Life

Less than a week later, BCEFA was asking me about my vision for this virtual show and my nerves were dialed to 11. Having never done anything like this before I felt a bit like a new saleswoman worried about hitting her first sales quota. So I started running my idea by other people in my industry to see what they thought, although not many of them understood. What was the connection between Broadway and my business? Did the Authentic Selling® community even like Broadway? These questions did not exactly help my nerves. But what all the feedback told me was I needed to get the Authentic Selling® language fixed. I had to get my language straightened out when I was explaining this special event. It dawned on me, I needed to create an Authentic Selling® Sales Map. And I was right, because I closed the biggest sale of my life. BCEFA was in, and we were going to create an incredibly special event.

One Night Only: A Musical Masterclass for a Cause

Ten months later, Authentic Selling® presented an unforgettable one-night-only event featuring a performance written, directed, and performed by Broadway legends. This unique musical celebration, in partnership with Broadway Cares and Kendrick Shope, was both a free show and an exclusive masterclass, showcasing 20 of the world's most talented Broadway stars, performers, and musicians. Not only did these performers captivate the audience with their singing, but they also shared invaluable insights on success, answering questions like:

- What does it take to succeed in your craft or business?
- How similar is the journey of a successful entrepreneur to that of an entertainer?
- What are the key pillars to being at the top of your industry?

Imagine having some of the world's greatest talent performing a private concert just for you. That night, Authentic Selling® raised $100,000 for BCEFA, providing support for numerous important causes. The event featured stars from *Scandal*, *Hamilton*, *Madame Secretary*, *Phantom of the Opera*, *Waitress*, *Wicked*, *A Chorus Line*, and future directors of *The Outsiders* and *The Wiz*. The evening was further enriched by a Broadway orchestra and a choreographer, all dedicated to inspiring the Authentic Selling® community.

In the most memorable moment for me personally, Joe McIntyre from New Kids On the Block introduced me to speak, before Halianna and I took the stage. This surprise, orchestrated by BCEFA, was something that touched the core of my very soul. That night is second only to moments with my daughter as the proudest moments of my life. In partnership with BCEFA, the small company I started offered our community a fresh way to create next-level moments for their audiences, helping them grow their online businesses in new and innovative ways.

That night we

- Honored the memory of a child who deeply touched Halianna's life.
- Raised $100,000 to support those in need, with donations providing essential services like meals for families facing food insecurity, medical treatment for those affected by HIV/AIDS, and heating for struggling families during the winter.

This once-in-a-lifetime event not only lifted up a community of business owners but also opened my eyes to new possibilities.

One Night Only happened about a year before my neurosurgery, and was a night that filled my soul with such happiness and pride. It was a shining light during one of the darkest times of my life.

A Lesson for You and Me Both

It doesn't matter what you're selling, you're going to have times when you find yourself flat on your face, and feel like giving up. Perseverance is having the strength to slow down without giving up. It's consistency. Notice consistency consistently shows up in all the Authentic Selling® Tools you've learned.

Your Own Authentic Selling® Journey

Before we move into your Authentic Selling® Business Plan, I will start with a genuine thank you for trusting me with your business. I understand how important it is for your business to succeed. Each tool, strategy, and process you've learned has been tested and only the proven best of the best made it in this book. It was important for me to be able to say to you, "As sure as my hair is red," this book has the power to change your business and also your life by providing you with an ick free way to make more money. Like it or not, money is the currency our world runs on, so it's important to have tools to help avoid financial stressors, give to your favorite charity, give your daughter a magical experience meeting her favorite Broadway star, or whatever makes your heart and soul sing.

By the time you read this, I will be close to sending my Halianna off to college and I can't even imagine my world without her in my house. Please check on me after she leaves! In similar fashion, it's now time to do the same with you and pass the power of the Authentic Selling® Tools, strategies, and processes onto you. My hope for you, beautiful human, is that Authentic Selling® changes your world as much as I have seen it improve the lives of my students, and impacts you in a positive way as much as it has for my family and me.

Just like I will do with Halianna, allow me to send you off to start your Authentic Selling® Journey with a few reminders. Anytime you feel sideways or if you've confused about what to do next, come back to the Authentic Selling® Foundations.

Authentic Selling® Foundations

- #1: Start with a genuine thank you. → Remember this if you're struggling to get started with any of the tools.
- #2: Selling must never feel icky, sleazy, slimy, or gross. If it does, stop and find another way. It's the Golden Rule of Authentic Selling® → Selling is helping, and anytime you do feel the ick, ask yourself how you can accomplish the same goal without feeling the ick.
- #3: Believe in the life-changing difference your product/service makes. If you don't, you'll struggle to sell it. You can use your Authentic Selling® Sales Map to be reminded of the true difference your work makes.
- #4: Create raving fans with every interaction, but don't be a doormat. Research shows these "soft skills" separate money-making businesses.
- #5: Follow-up is a must. It's proven to double businesses. So if constant follow-ups would feel icky for you, let's find an approach that doesn't.

Your Authentic Selling® Business Plan

1. Prospecting
2. Engagement
3. Understand the problem
4. Present the solution
5. Work through objections
6. Follow-up
7. Close
8. Results in revenue and raving fans

Prospecting

Authentic Selling® Prospecting involves actions that help new potential clients who might need what you're offering discover your business. It's about reaching out, chatting with people, and figuring out who might need what you're selling, so you can start a conversation and see if you can help them out.

Authentic Selling® Prospecting Tools

- Authentic Selling® Opt-in
- Authentic Selling® Headline Tool
- Authentic Selling® Fabulous Four Tool
- Authentic Selling® Social Media
- Authentic Selling® Sales Map

Pain Points Take-n-Tweak

- What do you want to change about your circumstances or reality?
- Utter lack of joy

- Constantly undermining your best intentions – setting a New Year's resolution but don't keep it
- Vicious cycles of self-guilt
- Ridding yourself of behaviors that interrupt the life you dream about
- Finding yourself in the same ole place
- Everyone teling you how lucky you are, you have a wonderful family, and beautiful kids
- Your happiness is created outside of you
- Continuing to experience difficulties over and over
- You may be happy but the real joy is missing
- Struggling to get unstuck
- Breaking the pattern of self-sabotage
- Your happiness is dependent on external factors
- Something isn't right
- Everything feels same ole same ole
- Something is missing
- Striving for more
- Striving to succeed
- Striving for excellence
- Stumbling on happiness instead of creating it
- One-third of people who suffer from depression are not helped by the standard treatment of pharmaceuticals and/or talk therapy
- Not all depression is the same
- Overcome feelings of helplessness and hopelessness

Benefits Take-n-Tweak

- Imagine the fresh possibilities
- Self-audit what's not working and begin a journey toward your "best life"

- Life is good, really good
- There is laughter in your life
- There is love in your life
- There is light and family
- There are long walks that feel like a fall afternoon
- Passion
- Perseverance
- The secret to _____
- Peak performance
- Personalized approach to _____
- Work smarter
- Live better
- Intervene in your own life and get more joy, meaning, purpose, etc.
- Invaluable guidance
- Change your life
- Healing depression
- A new way forward
- Whole person approach
- Lasting relief
- Find the missing puzzle pieces for your life. It could be the difference.
- Path to lasting joy
- How to negotiate a raise or contract
- Road map to making choices that help you live the life you want
- Simple tools you can use to get what you want
- Craft a persuasive message

- How to act boldly beyond your limits so that you're happier
- Take control of your career
- Alleviate allergies
- How to actually stick to new habits
- Turn your life around
- Real-world strategies for overcoming adversity
- Effective tips to increase your happiness
- Live your healthiest life
- Empower you to eat better
- Maximize your energy
- Become a better leader
- Tips to negotiate deals and contracts
- Get ahead in the workplace and life
- Fight cancer
- Dramatically improve your life
- Never slide backward again
- Develop a healthy lifestyle – no rigid dieting required
- Make choices that serve your desires
- Never feel I have to choke down healthy food again
- Live longer
- Make an unforgettable entrance
- Live cleaner
- Live happier
- Take control, prevent symptoms of illness
- Resources for all-around healthy living
- Relieve insomnia

- Skillfully communicate
- Get out of your own way
- Detox your environment
- The ultimate plan to health
- Lessen your risk for type 2 diabetes
- Balance your hormones including the stress hormone
- How to create glowing skin and mental clarity
- Replenish your mental, physical, and emotional energy
- Relieve headaches
- Expert recipes to help with skin disorders
- Simple, natural steps to feel better and healthier
- Steps to unlock your real motivation
- Better manage your time
- Put your professional future into your own hands
- Run more effective meetings
- Simple practical ways to eat healthy delicious food for life
- How to find your purpose and pursue your life's real work
- Discover your life's purpose
- Make willpower your secret weapon without becoming exhausted
- Inspiration to become who you're meant to be
- Practical help and inspiration to help you find the job you're meant to do
- Live a life that is connected, influential, and free
- Discover why you were placed on earth
- Do more than simply exist. Live.
- Honor your calling

Engagement

Authentic Selling® Engagement gets your prospect interested enough to click on a call to action. It's like having a conversation with someone. You want to keep people interested and involved, whether it's through chats, emails, or social media. You're building a connection, answering questions, and making sure they feel heard and understood. It's about making them feel excited and comfortable with you and your product.

Authentic Selling® Engagement Tools

- Authentic Selling® Social Media

Understand the Problem

Authentic Selling® Understanding the Problem is where you make your potential customers feel understood. You show prospects you're an expert and you not only understand but have empathy for their pain points. Think of it as getting on the same page with someone about what's bothering them.

Authentic Selling® Understand the Problem Tools

- Creating Authentic Selling® Pain Points
- Listening and Mirroring Your Clients Words
- Talk with five prospects a week on social media
- Authentic Selling® Sales Calls
- Authentic Selling® Copy
- Authentic Selling® From___To___Statement
  Step 1 → Insert product name or service

  Step 2 → from (insert your Authentic Selling® From statement)

  Step 3 → to (insert your Authentic Selling® To statement).

  "[Your product/service] will allow you to go from [pain point] to [benefit]."

Present the Solution

Following understanding your prospect's problem, you tell them what you're offering and show them how what you're offering can fix or make better the pain points prospects are dealing with. Presenting the solution is done in a simple, clear way to show how your product or service can make their life easier or better, and why it matters.

Authentic Selling® Present the Solutions Tools

- Authentic Selling® Sales Calls
- Authentic Selling® Sales Map

Features Take-n-Tweak

  - Coaching sessions
  - Classes
  - Video lessons
  - Meditations
  - Done for you assets
  - Facebook group
  - Book
- Authentic Selling® Copy
- Authentic Selling® From___To___Statement
  Step 1 → Insert product name or service
  Step 2 → from (insert your Authentic Selling® From statement)
  Step 3 → to (insert your Authentic Selling® To statement).
  "[Your product/service] will allow you to go from [pain point] to [benefit]."

Work Through Objections

This step in your Authentic Selling® Plan should feel like addressing your friend's concerns when they're unsure about something you're suggesting.

By listening to your prospect's worries or doubts, you can use objections to work for you as the seller. Objections are redirections giving you the opportunity to reassure your prospects and clear up any misunderstandings so they feel comfortable moving forward.

Authentic Selling® Working Through Objections Tools

Authentic Selling® Drive With Five Process For Working Through Potential Client Objections

- Step 1: Start With a Genuine Thank You
- Step 2: Tactical Empathy
- Step 3: Mirroring
- Step 4: Emotional Support Using Your Value Proposition
- Step 5: Choose one of the tools for working through objections/tools for closing
  - Tool 1: Let Them Off the Hook
  - Tool 2: Do Nothing and Sell in Follow-Up
  - Tool 3: Expert Recommendations
  - Tool 4: Make It Personal
  - Tool 5: Call Their Bluff
  - Tool 6: Head On
  - Tool 7: Discount the Objection
  - Tool 8: Back to Desire
  - Tool 9: Imagine
  - Tool 10: When Is a Good Time? (Great Tool for Corporate Selling or Telemarketing)
  - Tool 11: How to Get a Phone Number (Corporate Sales Tool)

Follow-Up

This step keeps you, your business, and offers relevant in your potential customer's mind. Think of follow-up as checking back with a friend after you've pitched weekend plans to the spa to see if they can come. Follow-up allows you to keep the conversation going, answering any last questions, and making sure they have everything they need to make a decision. Follow-up is something usually reserved for Upper Level Authentic Selling® but my Authentic Selling® Sales Guardrail wasn't comfortable holding off on Authentic Selling® Follow-Up Gems for you because follow-up is statistically proven to double your business. I could not let you go off into your own Authentic Selling® Journey without providing you with some Follow-Up Gems. When you use the Authentic Selling® Follow-Up Guidelines below, your follow-ups are going to be ick free and allow you to close more sales.

Authentic Selling® Follow-Up Tools

Follow-Up Guidelines

1. Start with a genuine but short thank you. People are limited on time and money so you want to show your appreciation while keeping them engaged
2. Have some empathy. All things being equal friends buy from friends. All things being unequal friends buy from friends. Gain some connection by understanding their struggle.
3. Compliment them.
4. Paint a vivid picture of why your customer needs your product. You might do this by revisiting the pain points of your customer. In other words, what are they struggling with or in need of so much that they would pay you for assistance.
5. Establish yourself as the expert. Tell them how and why you or your product is the answer to their problem/struggle.

6. Include proof. Include a testimonial from a satisfied customer to show that you can deliver what you promise. Statistics show that people don't click purchase because they don't believe you can deliver what you promise. Show them you can!

7. Call to action. All communication should have a call to action that entices the buyer to do something. Visit a page to learn more, make a purchase, or ask questions are examples of calls to action.

Close

Closing is when your potential customer is ready to say yes to your offers. A sale is closed when a payment or deposit is made and a contract is signed. It adds finality to the sales process so you can move onto delivering your product and changing the lives of your customers

Authentic Selling® Closing Tools

Calls to Action (CTA)

- Start your free trial today
- Try it free
- Get started
- Your next step to health begins here
- Your baby's sleep begins today
- Making money in your business starts here
- Learn more
- Learn how, here. It's free.
- Get started with your healthier lifestyle today
- A healthier lifestyle starts here
- Your next step to health begins here
- Experience the difference
- Next Steps

Enroll

OR

Have questions? Wonder if this is the right step for you? Email insert your email/contact info to get your questions answered.

- Next Steps

Fill out the application here. You will be contacted within 24 hours to schedule a no-obligation sales chat. Taking control of your business sales has never been so fun.

Let's get started.

- Next Steps

Schedule your no-obligation consult here. Taking control of your business sales has never been so fun. Let's get started.

Choose the Authentic Selling® University Plan That Works Best for You

One Payment of $4,000 USD	Four Monthly Payments of $1,000 USD	Ten Monthly Payments of $400 USD
Join now	Join now	Join now

- Ready to shortcut years of trying to figure out sales skills on your own by trial and error? Learn proven strategies to make sales with empathy and get real support from a sales expert every step of the way. Sales School is waiting for you.

There is a belief that once your business is successful enough, hits or exceeds quota, or makes enough money, things get easy. I would love for that to be true, but it's not the whole truth and too many people are out there pretending to be doing little to no work and making millions of dollars.

Authentic Selling® Truth → Someone is doing the work if a business is making money.

You Are Entering Your Best Era in Business Yet

The world needs what you have to offer. Every day your prospects are out there searching the internet, Googling, making phone calls, scouring social media looking for someone with your expertise who can improve their current pain points. Authentic Selling® will allow you to monetize your expertise while you make a positive impact on the lives of your customers.

This experience with you has been one of the best of my life, thank you. It felt important to me personally to share the vulnerable reality behind the journey that led Authentic Selling® to become the #1 sales process for your business. As embarrassing as some of what I shared was, I hope we all learned invaluable lessons from monumental failures that I wish I had learned before those mistakes were made. Even on your lowest day, as you pursue your very own remarkable goals and dreams, know that mind-blowing triumphs are waiting for you.

This is a story about making dreams come true, burning it all down, and finding truth.

What It Takes

You and I had what it takes to start a business, ready to take over the world, knowing that customers, money, and an extraordinary life were just around the corner. The first days as a business owner were a glorious, dream-filled, and scary-as-hell experience. Enduring all of the "what exactly is it you do" comments from our loved ones. (You've got a tool for that now inside this book!) Investing, investing, and investing countless dollars into our vision. Finding the nerve to believe we could create a business that could literally change our lives and the lives of others. Believing in the possibility of our businesses to create the freedom to do more of what we love (spending time with our kids, traveling, or even retiring early).

But long before the dream business, comes the courage to just get started. In an instant, we dared to make a different choice and if it all ended tomorrow at least we had the courage to say no to the status quo.

Be proud that we are braver than our neighbors who are playing it safe but are miserable. Once the passion for truth, beauty, freedom, and the dream is ignited in us, it feels like we have no choice but to run toward that passion and possibility. Yes, we may have to make a few mistakes along the way, myself more than most! The support of Authentic Selling® students, clients, and community, my friends, and family kept me going enough to go from the "Down the Rabbit Hole of Despair Era" to emerge to "My Best Era in Business Yet."

You and I may be on opposite sides of the globe and unfortunately, we may never meet but knowing there are other humans like us, who are brave enough to fight for a different life, feeling the energy of your existence every day, allows me to believe in better.

It is an honor living, breathing, and working in the space with you.

This is a story about beauty. This is a story about YOU.

Now it is my honor to invite you as you begin your very own Authentic Selling® Journey to take this leap into "Your Best Era in Business Yet" with me. I believe there isn't much that will stop you from succeeding and with the right plan you're going to accomplish more than you dreamed was possible.

I believe in you and I believe in your business,

Kendrick

Acknowledgments

A genuine thank you to:

Keith Shope Sr., Dad, you taught me the true meaning of family, pushed me toward excellence, and always demanded good citizenship!

Judy Sherlin Shope, Mom, your unwavering support, boundless patience, and belief have been my guiding light throughout this journey. This book is as much a reflection of the endless love you give to me as it is of my dreams.

Keith Shope Jr., my brother, you have the biggest heart. The memories I have with you are some of the stories that light my way when the world goes sideways.

Donna Shope, my sister-in-law, you made me feel "normal" when I saw how hard you love Hadley and you also make life brighter and more fun.

My husband, Blake, you bring laughter into our lives and stand by Halianna and me through every Broadway show, NYC trip, and wild idea. And to your family, Alan, Linda, Brooks, and Angela for accepting me, making me one of you, and loving me.

My two best friends, Addey, my bury a body person for life, and Jenny, who is with me through the best and the absolute worst times and loves me unconditionally.

Anna Lora, you are the closest thing I have to a sister, my world is brighter and better since the day you were born.

Hadley, my niece, you make me smile every time I see your beautiful face. Will you add my book to your unofficial library?

Addison, Austin, Emma, Liz, Henry, Frankie, Cameron, Mattie Jane, Cruz, Sophie, Skyler, and Piper, always believe in your dreams.

To my first-ever crush, Jason Bruce, for being 18 when I was 13 and never making me feel embarrassed, even when I was *very* embarrassing. Thanks for helping me believe in my future (and that restraining orders might be a real concern). If you're reading this, I swear I've matured. Mostly. 😉

To my second-ever crush, Joey McIntyre, the night you introduced me at the Broadway Cares charity event, you made a childhood dream real! I fell in love with New Kids On The Block 39 years ago and have been a Blockhead ever since.

Robin Talent, how did I ever function without your genius and friendship? Your love, patience, and ability to pick me up when I melt into a puddle of tears is nothing short of magic.

Meghan Stevenson, we did it! The incredible people at Wiley and my agent, Steve at Folio Lit, for surviving the ID Theft apocalypse with me. Julie Kerr, the best developmental editor in the galaxy. Deborah Williams, who had the unfortunate task of teaching me to use Microsoft Word! This book would not have been possible without all the brilliance you each poured into this book, thank you!

Holly Ostrout, thank you for teaching me how to even begin to draft a book and for being one of the brightest lights in my business world. Melissa Burkheimer, you poured into my business with your creative genius and being the best designer and branding expert on the planet.

Brandi Bernoskie, Vanessa V. Lewis, Doug Richesin, your kindness, and willingness to go through the hell that was this past year, is one of the reasons I'm still standing!

Patrick McCray, you are one of the most gifted directors and creatives. Thanks for believing in me and forgiving all the missed dinners. Share YOUR story, the world is waiting for it.

The city of Sweetwater, Tennessee, my home, where these wild dreams took root, and to Nancy Cason, who put me on a stage for the first time, nurturing a love of the stage. You gave me one of the best gifts in my life, creating a life-long love of the stage; you changed my entire world.

Tammy Lee, the genius photographer who made me feel beautiful despite all the hot flashes and pounds!

A special thank you to Brenda Bryan of the Lily Pad Boutique for the style, confidence, and love from day one.

Papa Joe, I regret you did not get to read this book, thank you for instilling a love of reading in me that has expanded my world since I was a toddler.

Finally, Broadway Cares Equity Fights AIDS, Susan Slotoroff, Jenna Adamek, Danny Whitman, and Tom Viola, you accepted us into the BCEFA family, allowing Halianna and me to be a part of the "philanthropic heart" of Broadway.

NYC, I have never felt safer than when I smell the trash, hear the roar of traffic, and see the rush of people, you are my home away from home.

About the Author

Kendrick Shope is an internationally recognized sales expert and the leading female figure in the world of sales. After a distinguished career as a top performer at three Fortune 500 companies, Kendrick traded in her Manolo's when she left the corporate scene to shake up the sales training industry. She created Authentic Selling®, the #1 online sales training program, which has helped thousands of clients, students, and corporations earn millions of dollars in revenue.

Kendrick's insights have been featured on popular platforms like *The Steve Harvey Show*, NBC, ABC, *Reader's Digest*, *Headline News*, *The Advocate*, *The Daily Times*, and more.

Authentic Selling® changes the icky, sleazy, slimly, old way of selling by focusing on authenticity, with the belief that selling is helping. Kendrick's unique, integrity-based approach not only delivers impressive results but has also been embraced by companies to increase revenue, build strong partnerships, and motivate teams to achieve new levels of success.

Authentic Selling® combines her sweet as pie but tough as nails no-nonsense attitude, teaching people how to smash their goals without sacrificing their values. The results speak for themselves: breaking through past performance barriers, doubling, and even tripling revenues.

You are just as likely to find Kendrick and her daughter soaking up the talent on Broadway in NYC, volunteering for their favorite charity, Broadway Cares Equity Fights AIDS, or with earphones blocking out the world listening to the newest book on Audible. Kendrick is a third-generation graduate of the University of Tennessee, Knoxville, and loves attending "Football time in Tennessee" with her incredible family.

Index

action
  in AIDA, 115
  see also Call to Action (CTA)
AIDA (Attention, Interest, Desire, Action), 115
And Just Like That, 112
attention
  in AIDA, 115
  of competitive expert buyers, 165–6
  Opt-In content to get, 171
  sales language to get, 169
  Sales Page copy to get, 116–17, 119, 121, 123, 126, 131, 136, 142, 146, 152–3
  attention getting statements, 161
    see also Opt-Ins
Authentic Selling®, ix–xxix
  business development with, 47–61
  business plan for, 185–205
  closing in, 91–108
  communication in, 63–76
  customization in, 186
  foundations of, 3–12
  gratitude in, xi–xii
  life balance in, xii
  mindset for, 1–13
  money and time in, xii–xiv
  old way of selling vs., 20–1
  during pandemic, 186–7
  prospecting methods in, 161–84
  sales conversations in, 77–89
  Sales Page copy in, 109–61
  Shope sales stories about, xxi–xxix
  uniqueness of, xiv
  Upper Level, 189
  your customer's money in, 15–30
  Your Fabulous Four in, xv–xx
  see also individual topics
Authentic Selling® Definitions
Authentic Selling® Placebo Effect, 77
crickets, 180–1
hook, record scratch moment, attention getting statement, and headline, 161
Marketing Vortex, xvi
pain point, 50
selling, 78
Villain, 63, 64

213

Authentic Selling® Double D's, xvi–xvii
Authentic Selling® Foundations, 3–13, 193
   believe in life-changing difference your product or service makes, 8–9, 193
   create a raving fan with every interaction, but don't be a doormat, 9–10, 193
   follow-up is a MUST, 10–12, 193
   presidential candidates' reliance on, 168
   selling should never feel icky, sleazy, slimy, or gross, 7–8, 193
   starting with genuine thank you, 4–7, 193
Authentic Selling® Math
   on asking to share positive experiences, 31
   of create raving fans, 9–10
   number of silent closes, 118
   on social media messages, 31
Authentic Selling® Placebo Effect, 77
Authentic Selling® Prospecting Methods
   email signature, 181–2
   Opt-In, 168–79
   social media, 179–1
Authentic Selling® Pro Tips
   caring about prospects and customers, xix
   "diagnosing" customers, 49
   finding the actual meaning of something, xii–xiii
   investment, 139
   lack of testimonials, 148
   observing industry leaders' content, 173–4
   Opt-Ins, 168–9, 171–2
   past testimonials, 122
   prices, 140
   promise of what product or service will do, 123
   Sales Page copy, 109
   storing prospecting, 178–9
   telling your story, 135
   using Authentic Selling®, xix
   why somebody is going to choose you, 134
   word of mouth is best form of advertising, 32
   writing about features and benefits, 129–30
Authentic Selling® Real Talk, on sales calls, 129
Authentic Selling® Sales Guardrail, xiv, 12, 161, 185–6
Authentic Selling® Sales Tools
   for business development, 61
   Sales Map, 50 (*see also* Sales Map)
   for understanding your customer's money mindset, 30
   see also specific tools and topics
Authentic Selling® Tools

for benefits, 63–5 (*see also* communication)
for closing, 203
for communication, 69–76
Double D's, xvi–xvii
Drive With Five, 100–8
for engagement, 199
for follow-up, 202
for headlines, 181–2
for presenting the solutions, 200
for prospecting, 183–4, 194–198
for sales conversations, 107–8
selling is helping, 13
for understanding the problem, 199
for working through objections, 201
Writing Emails That Convert, 173
Your Fabulous Four, xv–xx
see also specific tools and topics
Authentic Selling® Truths
in building positive customer relationships authentically, 31–46 (*see also* relationship building)
definition of the word selling, xii
doing the work for business to make money, 204
don't make outrageous claims, 122
lack of trust, time, need are among top objections, 31
potential customers want to buy from experts, 48

reading sales pages, 120
sales conversation is not a bait and switch, 82
simple does not mean easy, 111
take care of prospects' hesitations with integrity, 99
Authentic Selling® University payment plan, 119, 145, 149, 151, 157, 204
Authentic Selling® Vocabulary Words, 91
Authentic Selling® Vulnerability Tool, 189–90
Authentic Selling® Warning, about Vulnerability tool, 190

Baskin Robbins, 168
BCEFA (Broadway Cares/Equity Fights AIDS), 112–13, 187–90
Beck, Martha, 58, 74
Belgray, Laura, 135
belief(s)
of customer, challenging, 20–1
in life-changing difference of your product or service, 8–9, 27–8
in what you're selling, xvii
in yourself, xviii
benefit(s)
Authentic Selling® Benefits tools, 64
challenge of learning, 63–4
happiness as, 76

benefit(s) (*continued*)
  identifying, 51–2
  moving from pain points to, 86
  pattern interrupt with, 86
  presenting features with, 129
  on Sales Map, 66–9, 75–6
  in Sales Page copy, 128–31, 133–4, 144, 147–8, 154–7
  Take-n-Tweak for, 53–6, 66–8, 195–8
  for values-based buyers, 165
better version of yourself, being a, 56–8
Bid Ed's Pizza, 9
blogs
  Call to Action for Opt-Ins for, 177
  see also social media prospecting
Bon Jovi, Jon, xii
Broadway Backwards, 112–13
Broadway Cares/Equity Fights AIDS (BCEFA), 112–13, 187–90
bullets, paragraphs vs., 120
business development, 47–61
  and being a better version of yourself, 56–8
  definitions in Authentic Selling®, 50–2
  diagnosing your customers, 49–50
  and expertise, 48–9
  mastermind experience in, 58–60
  Sales Map for, 50, 52–6
  see also prospecting
Business Plan, 185–205

Authentic Selling® Foundations for, 194
  for closing, 203–4
  for engagement, 199
  for follow-up, 202–3
  and One Night Only event, 187–92
  for presenting the solution, 200
  for prospecting, 194–8
  and Sales Guardrail, 185–6
  for understanding the problem, 199
  for working through objections, 200–1
Buyer Psychology Colors, 164–6
buyers
  categories of, 164–6
  finding people happy to buy from you, 167–8 (*see also* prospecting)
  journey of (*see* customer journey triangle)
  money of (*see* customer's money)
buying
  emotions vs. logic in, 42–5
  from friends, 32, 45–6, 168
  understanding prospect's brain in (*see* prospecting)
Buy Me Now statement, 145–6, 149, 157

Call to Action (CTA)
  for One Night Only event, 189
  of Opt-Ins, 177–8

on Sales Page, 139–42, 145
Caraway, Ed, 11, 17
cautious buyers (blue), 165
closing, 86–7, 91–108
    in Business Plan, 203–4
    Drive With Five in, 100–8
    and five things that stop a sale, 97
    and meddling with customer's money, 96–7
    most dreaded words in, 92
    in sales conversations, 92–3
    Shope sales story of, 93–5, 98–9
    silent closes, 118, 120
    tools for overcoming objections in, 104–7
    use of shame and guilt in, 95–6
common things, done uncommonly well, 9–10
communication, 63–76
    close to Sales Guardrail, 12
    5 Senses Tool in, 74–6
    and happiness as a benefit, 76
    importance of benefits tools in, 64
    importance of words in, 1–3, 63–4
    normal rules of conversation in, 64–5
    with potential buyers (*see* prospecting)
    of product or service value, 28–30
    sales conversations, 77–89
    sales language, 169
    and Sales Map benefits, 66–9
    and Sales Map pain points, 65–6
    Shope sales story of, 72–3
    To ___ Statements in, 66
    From ___ To ___ Statement in, 69–71
    Villain Tool in, 73–4
    written, 109 (*see also* Sales Page copy)
competitive expert buyers (red), 165–6
confidence, lack of, 98
confrontational selling, 16–17, 20
connections, making, 83–4 *see also* relationship building
consistency
    in creating content, 181
    perseverance as, 192
    and trust, 11
content
    creating, 172–3
    deep vs. wide, 172–3
    of Opt-Ins, 171–4 (*see also* Opt-Ins)
    on Sales Page (*see* Sales Page copy)
copywriters, frequently asked questions about, 159
crickets, 180–1
CTA *see* Call to Action
customer journey triangle, 38–40
    applying, 39–40
    example of, 41–2
    stages in, 38–42
customer service, 9

customer's mindset, 26–30
customer's money, 15–30
   and Authentic Selling® approach, 17–18
   customer's mindset about, 26–30
   and getting thrown out of the office, 16–17
   and moving the sale forward, 19
   as none of your business, 96–7
   and old way of selling vs. Authentic Selling® way, 20–1
   Sales Tools for, 26–30
   and selling technique, 15–16
   and value to the customer, 21–6
   and your right to sell, 18–19

data
   with competitive expert buyers, 165, 166
   for introvert buyers, 165
   with ready-to-buy fan buyers, 166
decision making, during crises, 34–5
deep content, wide content vs., 172–3
desire
   in AIDA, 115
   Sales Page copy to create, 122–4, 127–8, 137, 143, 147, 153–4
diagnosing your customers, 49–50
difference your product or service makes, believing in, 8–9, 27–8

Disney Cruises, 10
Double D's, xvi–xvii
doubt, 91
Dr. Dre, 118
Drive With Five, 100–8
   Mirroring in, 102–3
   Tactical Empathy in, 101
   "thank you" in, 100–1
   value proposition in, 103–4
   for working through potential client objections, 104–7, 201

emails
   for One Night Only event, 188–9
   that convert, 172–3
email signature, 181–2
emotional appeals, balancing logical appeals and, 42–5
engagement, in Business Plan, 199
expectations, setting, 84
expertise, 28, 48–9

FAQs (frequently asked questions), 158–60
features
   identifying, 51
   in keeping prospect's attention, 85–6
   presenting benefits with, 129
   in Sales Map, 50
   in Sales Page copy, 128–31, 133–4, 144, 147–8, 154–7
   Take-n-Tweak for, 53
   see also product or service

Finding Your Own Northstar (Beck), 58
5 Senses Tool, 74–6
follow-up
    in Business Plan, 202–3
    as a foundation, 10–12
Ford, Henry, 10
Forleo, Marie, 58–9, 72
freebies, 168 *see also* Opt-Ins
"free" calls, 80
frequently asked questions (FAQs), 158–60
friends, buying from, 32, 45–6, 168 *see also* relationship building
From ___ To ___ Statements, 69–71, 76

Georgia Pacific, 8, 11–12, 41–2
getting thrown out of the office, 16–17
Girish, Uma, 158
goal of sales calls, 87
Golden Rule of selling, 7–8
good things, too much of, 78–81
gratitude, xi–xii, 4–7, 83
guilt, used as tool, 95–6

happiness, as a benefit, 76
hard opt-ins, 170
headlines, 161, 169, 174–6 *see also* Opt-Ins
helping, selling as, 1–3
Hightower, Carla, 157

Hinkel, Stacey, 113
homework, frequently asked questions about, 160
hook, 117, 161, 169 *see also* Opt-Ins
How-To titles (Opt-Ins), 175

"I can't afford it," 21–2, 25–7, 92
ideal client, finding, 47–8 *see also* business development
Informational titles (Opt-Ins), 176
inspiration, for creating content, 181
interest
    in AIDA, 115
    Sales Page copy to create, 117–21, 123–4, 126–7, 131–2, 136, 142, 146, 153
introvert buyers (blue), 165
investment
    frequently asked questions about, 158
    Sales Page copy about, 139–40, 145
    sharing, in sales conversations, 86

K.I.S.S. Tool, 110–15, 170
Kiss Principle, 110, 111
knowing your customer, 32–7, 47–8
Kobuke, Jo Ann, 157

LaPorte, Danielle, 59, 71
leading by example, 11
life
    balance in, xii
    preciousness of, 37

listening, 87
lizard brain, 74
logical appeals, balancing emotional appeals and, 42–5

Marketing Vortex, xvi
McIntyre, Joe/Joey, 23, 71, 191
mindset, 1–13
   of customer, 26–30
   and foundations of Authentic Selling®, 3–12
   and Sales Guardrail, 12
   of selling as helping, 1–3
Mirroring, 85, 87, 102–3
modality, for opt-ins, 170–1
money
   in Authentic Selling®, xiv
   customer's mindset about, 26–30 (*see also* customer's money)
   in selling, xii–xiv
   tools for using/managing, 192–3
   trumped by value, 21–2
Moulin Rouge The Musical, 112
moving sales forward, 19
multitasking, 110

New Kids on the Block, 23, 71, 166
niche, frequently asked questions about, 159
Nordstrom, 170
Number titles (Opt-Ins), 174

objections
   addressing, in sales conversations, 86
   common, 97
   defined, 91
   "I can't afford it," 21–2, 25–7
   overcoming, 104–7
   working through, 200–1
One Night Only event, 187–92
Opt-Ins, 168–79
   Call to Action of, 177–8
   content of, 171–4
   creating trust with, 178–9
   email links to, 181
   modality for, 170–1
   for One Night Only event, 189
   title of, 174–6
   types of, 169–70

pain points
   defined, 50–1
   getting to, 84
   identifying, 51
   moving to benefits from, 86
   in Sales Map, 50
   Sales Page questions about, 119
   sharing, 77
   Take-n-Tweak for, 52–3, 65–6, 194–5
paragraphs, bullets vs., 120
pattern interrupt
   with benefits, 86
   with features, 85–6
payment plan, for Authentic Selling® University, 119, 145, 149, 151, 157, 204
perseverance, 192
pink spoon, 168 *see also* Opt-Ins

placebo effect, 77–81
podcasts
    Call to Action for Opt-Ins for, 177
    see also social media prospecting
The Polar Express, xxvi–xvii
possibilities, transition to *see* Transition to What's Possible
Pottery Barn, 170
practicing sales calls, 87–8
presenting the solution, in Business Plan, 200
presidential candidates, 167–8
price(s)
    being firm on, 25
    on website, 139–40
problem aware stage (customer journey), 38–41
product or service
    believing in difference made by, 8–9, 27–8
    frequently asked questions about, 160
    going into debt for, 27–30
    main question to ask about, 15–16
    Sales Page copy about (*see* Sales Page copy)
    that exceeds expectations, 9
    value of, to customer, 21–6
    value proposition for, 103–4
prospecting, 161–84
    in Business Plan, 194–198
    and categories of buyers, 164–6
    and email signature, 181–2
    finding people happy to buy from you, 167–8
    importance of understanding buyer's brain, 163–4
    Opt-In method, 168–79
    places for, 182–3
    on social media, 179–1

QR code opt-ins, 170
questions, as sales conversation step, 86
Question titles (Opt-Ins), 176, 180

Radomski, Michelle, 158
raving fans
    creating, 9–10
    as ready-to-buy, 166
    as stage in customer journey, 38–41
Reader Responsibility titles (Opt-Ins), 175
ready-to-buy fan buyers (white), 166
record scratch moments, 161, 171
    see also Opt-Ins
relationship building, 31–46
    and buying off of emotions while justifying with logic, 42–5
    customer journey triangle in, 38–40

relationship building (*continued*)
   and how well you know your customer, 32–7
   importance of, 31–2
   power of stories in, 44–5
   and stages of customer journey, 40–2
results
   desire for, 129
   frequently asked questions about, 158–9
   in Sales Page copy, 149–52, 157–8
Rich Happy & Hot Live, 58–9

sales conversations, 77–89
   anatomy of, 92–3
   bait and switch, 82
   closes for (*see* closing)
   defined, 81–3
   formula/script for, 80–1
   "free" calls, 80
   important aspects of, 87–8
   key actions for, 88
   successful, 99
   taking control of, 80
   that convert, steps in, 83–7, 89
   and too much of a good thing, 78–81
Sales Guardrail, xiv, 12
   and blind contacts, 161
   checking in with, 185–6
sales language, 169
Sales Map, 50, 52–6
   benefits on, 66–9, 75–6
   features on, 50, 51
   for One Night Only event, 190
   pain points on, 50, 65–6
   as scroll disruptor, 169
   in writing Sales Page copy, 110
   see also business development
Sales Page copy, 109–61
   AIDA for, 115
   Buy Me Now statement in, 145–6
   to create desire, 122–4
   to create interest, 117–20
   and customer's time constraints, 110
   examples of, 131–4, 136–9, 142–9, 152–60
   features + benefits in, 128–31
   formula for, 152
   frequently asked questions section in, 162
   to grab attention, 116–17
   Investment/Call to Action in, 139–42
   K.I.S.S. Tool for, 110–11
   results and testimonials in, 149–52
   Shope sales story for, 111–15
   Transitioning to What's Possible in, 120–2
   Transition to Trust in, 125–8
   Why You Statement in, 134–6
Sales School
   examples of Sales Page copy about, 130–4, 138–9, 144–5, 147–8, 154–6

frequently asked questions about, 158–60
payment plan for, 119, 145, 149, 151, 157
purpose of, 128
scripts, 80–1
practicing, 87–8
see also sales conversations
selling
confrontational, 16–17, 20–1
definition of, xii, xiii, 78
getting thrown out of the office when, 16–17
as helping, 1–3
icky, sleazy, slimy, or gross, 6–8, 95–6
learning something to move sales forward, 19
main question to ask about, 15–16
new definition of, xiv
old way vs. Authentic Selling®, 20–1
placebo effect in, 78–81
relational, 31 (*see also* relationship building)
as step in sales conversations, 85
things that stop a sale, 97
using guilt or shame in, 95–6
usual perception of, xi
your right to, 18–19
see also sales conversations
services offered *see* product or service

shame, used as tool, 95–6
She Rocks @ College, 162–3
Shih, Jenny, 57–8, 60, 61, 72–3
silent closes, 118, 120
Slottoroff, Susan, 189
social butterfly buyers (yellow), 164
social media prospecting, 179–81
avoiding pitfalls of, 181
Call to Action for Opt-Ins in, 177
importance of, 179–80
storing prospects from, 178–9
soft opt-ins, 169
solution aware stage (customer journey), 38–41
Steering by Starlight (Beck), 74
Steve Harvey Show, 78–9
stories
on "About" page, 135
with competitive expert buyers, 165
power of, 44–5
with ready-to-buy fan buyers, 166
with social butterfly buyers, 164
surprising and delighting customers, 9–10

Tactical Empathy, 85, 87, 101
testimonials
with competitive expert buyers, 165
for introvert buyers, 165
in Sales Page copy, 149–52, 157–8

text opt-ins, 170
"thank you," 4–7
    at beginning of sales conversations, 83
    in Drive With Five, 100–1
    when prospect shares something personal, 85
time
    customers' constraints with, 110
    in selling, xii–xiv
title of Opt-Ins, 174–6
too much of a good thing, 78–81
To ___ Statements, 66
trailer, 117
training, frequently asked questions about, 160
Transition to Trust, 125–8, 132–3, 137–8, 143–4, 147, 154
Transition to What's Possible, 120–2, 124, 127, 132, 137, 143, 146, 153
trust
    created with Opt-Ins, 178–9
    lack of, 10–11
    Sales Page copy transitioning to (*see* Transition to Trust)
    when you take care of prospects' hesitations with integrity, 99
Tveit, Aaron, 112

unaware stage (customer journey), 38–41
understanding
    of the buyer's brain, 163–4
    in conversations, 87
    of the problem, 199
    of your customer's money mindset, 30
Upper Level Authentic Selling®, 189

value of product or service
    communicating, 28–30
    to the customer, 21–6
value proposition, 103–4
values
    with competitive expert buyers, 165, 166
    defined, 91
    with ready-to-buy fan buyers, 166
values-based buyers (green), 165
Vanguard, 170
Villain, 63, 64
Villain Tool, 73–4, 76
Vulnerability Tool, 189–90

what's possible, transition to *see* Transition to What's Possible
Why You Statement, 134–6, 139, 148–9, 155–6
wide content, deep content vs., 172–3
word of mouth advertising, 32
words
    importance of, 2–3, 63–4
    sales language, 169
    see also communication

Writing Emails That Convert, 173
written communication, 109 *see also* Sales Page copy

York, Dr., 113–14
Your Fabulous Four, xv–xx
   importance of, xv
   steps in creating, xvi–xx
   where to use, xx
YouTube videos
   Call to Action for Opt-Ins for, 177
   see also social media prospecting

Ziglar, Zig, 28, 97